Tabernacle Stories of Faith

Snapshots of God's faithfulness to His people at Tabernacle Baptist Church.
Cartersville, Georgia

Compiled by Kim Lewis and Denise Hamilton

Forward by Dr. Don Hattaway Senior Pastor

Copyright © 2007
by Kim Lewis and Denise Hamilton

Tabernacle Stories of Faith
Snapshots of God's faithfulness to His people at Tabernacle Baptist Church. Cartersville, Georgia
by Kim Lewis and Denise Hamilton

Printed in the United States of America

ISBN 978-1-60477-326-2

All rights reserved solely by the author. The author guarantees all contents are original and do not infringe upon the legal rights of any other person or work. No part of this book may be reproduced in any form without the permission of the author. The views expressed in this book are not necessarily those of the publisher.

Unless otherwise indicated, Bible quotations are taken from *The Holy Bible, New International Version, (NIV)*. Copyright © 1973, 1978, 1984 by International Bible Society. Used by permission of Zondervan Publishing House.

Other scripture quotations are taken from:

The Holy Bible, King James Version Copyright © 1979, 1980, 1982 Thomas Nelson, Inc. Publishers, Nashville, TN

The Holy Bible, Amplified Version, 1965 by Zondervan Publishing House. All rights reserved.

The Holy Bible, The Message taken from www.biblegateway.org accessed September 1, 2007 through September 30, 2007

The New American Standard Version taken from www.biblegateway.org accessed September 1, 2007 through September, 2007

Please visit our church website at www.tabernaclebaptist.org

www.xulonpress.com

*This will be for the Lord's renown,
for an everlasting sign,
which will not be destroyed.
Isaiah 55:13b*

*They overcame him (Satan)
by the blood of the Lamb
and the word of their testimony.
Revelation 12:11*

TABLE OF CONTENTS

Forward – Pastor Don Hattaway 11
Introduction – Kim Lewis 13
Church History 19

Stories of Faith

1 – Nick Adams 25
2 – Lisa Bagnell 27
3 – Lisa Bandy 37
4 – Gayle Beck 41
5 – Darlene Benton 45
6 – Ed Bruce 47
7 – Judy Bruce 49
8 – Louise Dee 51
9 – Anne Donahoo 57
10 – Betty Faile 61
11 – Bertha Fontaine 65
12 – Sherry Glaze 69
13 – Wanda Gray 77
14 – John Gresh 83

15 – Susan Hatfield	87
16 – Don Hattaway	91
17 – Sonny Hattaway	95
18 – Sue Hedden	99
19 – Nancy Higginbotham	103
20 – Jennie Horton	107
21 – Kathy Howren	113
22 – Kathy Howren	117
23 – Caren Kelley	123
24 – Darla LaRue	127
25 – Mike LaRue	135
26 – Kim Lewis	147
27 – Judy Little	157
28 – Becky McCrory	161
29 – Susan May	167
30 – Julie Mitchell	171
31 – Holly Muntz	179
32 – Kathy Olivet	183
33 – Chris Overvold	187
34 – Sheila Parker	191
35 – Libby Beasley-Perdue	195
36 – Nancy Pohl	197
37 – Charles Puckett	203
38 – Lydia Quillen	207
39 – Dawn Rockey	211
40 – Jimmy Scroggins	215
41 – Jimmy Scroggins	219
42 – Arleen Shook	223
43 – Cindy Smith	229
44 – J.B. and Judy Smith	233
45 – Rod Strickland	239
46 – Ric and Andrea Sundstrom	245

47 – Jean Tatum 249
48 – Max Tatum 253
49 – Sandy Taylor 255
50 – Jonathan Tipper 261
51 – J.E. Tumlin 269
52 – Ann Wood 273

Appendix – Billy Graham, Plan of Salvation 277

FORWARD
by
Dr. DON HATTAWAY
SENIOR PASTOR

Some news is just too good to keep to yourself. This is especially true regarding news of God's blessings in the lives of believers. This book is a collection of testimonies that tells how God has worked among His people. Every story recorded within the pages of this work serves to bear witness of the faithfulness, grace, and power of God.

The purpose for this book is multi-faceted. **First,** we aim to glorify our Lord and Savior Jesus Christ. We want the entire world to know that in spite of the lost condition of humankind, salvation has been made available through faith in the sinless Savior. God has promised to forgive all who confess their sins and trust in the sacrificial death and glorious resurrection of His Son, Jesus.

Secondly, this book is intended to encourage those who have grown discouraged from the difficulties and demands of life. There are many challenges to be faced on our journey of faith. Sometimes it is hard to understand the pain and sorrows that accompany this life. That's why it is good to read how God has provided for others in times of despair. In learning how others have weathered the storms of life, we can be encouraged that God will also see us through the turbulent waters ahead.

And finally – joy. Joy is another reason this collection of testimonies has been written. Our world is filled with bad news. Everywhere we turn we are exposed to messages of defeat. These real life stories are filled with victory and hope. They record the age-old truth that God's people are not forsaken. Through these testimonies you will see that the real source of joy is found in a committed relationship with God through His Son, the Lord Jesus.

As you read through the pages of this collection, remember that God is at work in the lives of His people. His power and presence are just as real in your life as they were in the lives of those recorded in this book. Realizing this truth, let your life be a living testimony of His grace and mercy to those around you.

INTRODUCTION
by
KIM LEWIS

I have always loved the old hymn, "Blessed Assurance."

Blessed assurance, Jesus is mine!
O what a foretaste of glory divine!
Heir of salvation, purchase of God,
born of his Spirit, washed in his blood.

Refrain:
This is my story, this is my song,
praising my Savior all the day long;
this is my story, this is my song,
praising my Savior all the day long.
Perfect submission, perfect delight,
visions of rapture now burst on my sight;
angels descending bring from above
echoes of mercy, whispers of love.

> *Perfect submission, all is at rest;*
> *I in my Savior am happy and blest,*
> *watching and waiting, looking above,*
> *filled with his goodness, lost in his love.*[1]

These lyrics were penned by Fannie Crosby who, as a 6 week old infant, was struck with an illness which left her permanently blind. She had every reason to embrace bitterness, but she refused. As a result, her life became a beautiful story of the love and grace of God. She gave herself tirelessly to serving others when she herself had every right to be served. As a result, God allowed her to write more than 9,000 hymns which have blessed generations of Christians. Fannie Crosby's life was not easy, but she found purpose and beauty in serving the God who created her.

Every time I sing that hymn, I think about the fact that everyone has a story. Not necessarily a pretty one or an easy one, but a story that belongs to them. A unique story of the details of their life and the workings of God in and through their circumstances as He takes the natural and does something supernatural.

As I sat through the Thanksgiving service at Tabernacle Baptist Church in 2006, our pastor, Dr. Don Hattaway, encouraged us to do something different. He told us that this service would be a true time of personal thanksgiving. A time where we, as the congregation, could stand up and give a personal word of praise and thanks to God for His goodness and provision to us over the year(s). And so, one by one, individuals stood up in their pews and gave a brief testimony about what God had done in their lives and how grateful they were to Him. It was a sweet time. It was a time of sharing stories…stories of faith.

I remember thinking to myself, "I wish everyone in the church was here so they could hear for themselves the amazing things God has done in the lives of these people!" Let me stress, these were not testimonies from the staff or seminary graduates, though their stories are equally amazing. No, these were teachers, businessmen and women, grandpas, grandmas, moms and dads. By the time I reached my car, I had an idea. The thought sounded something like this, "Write their stories so everyone will know." My first reaction was, "Wait a minute. Was this my idea or God's?" I had 3 young boys at home and a full plate already. When would I do this and how on earth would I ever approach such a big project? I was totally unqualified. So, I dismissed the thought…but it kept returning.

Not coincidentally, I began taking a Bible study on Wednesday nights by Priscilla Shirer, *Discerning the Voice of God*. As I sat spellbound by each week's lesson of in-depth Scripture and teaching, I began to hear that "still small voice" referred to in **I Kings 19:12**. As the idea to write these stories continued to swirl around in my head, I became increasingly frustrated. I woke up one particular day with a "this is it" attitude. I knew I needed to concede to this as the prodding of the Holy Spirit or dismiss it as my own idea. Today would be the day.

As I approached my Bible time that morning, I specifically asked the Lord to confirm this idea, either way, through His Word. As I turned in my Bible, the pages literally fell open to **Psalms 102**. I gasped as the first verse I read said this, (**verse 18**) *"Let this be written for a future generation, that a people not yet created may praise the Lord."* As if that were not enough, I received a second confirmation through **Isaiah 30:8**,*"Now go and write down these **words**. Write them in a **book**. They will stand until the end of time as a witness."* (emphasis added) Okay Lord. I get the picture. That is how it all began.

You may be reading this book as one who submitted a personal story or as a family member or friend. On the other hand, you may not know any of these precious people. Either way, I assure you that their stories will speak volumes to you.

It is my firm belief that God, the God Who created you and Who is intimately aware of all you are going through, (see **Psalm 100:3** and **Jeremiah 29:11**) has led you to read these stories as a means of encouragement or better yet, salvation through a personal relationship with Him.

Perhaps you will be able to identify with one of the many struggles shared in these pages and find strength and support as you endure your own test or trial. Or maybe you have never really believed that God is real or that He is available to you by faith in Jesus Christ. (**I John 1:7-9**) Whatever your story or place in life, it is my prayer that God will meet you here, in the midst of these stories…stories of ordinary lives and imperfect people through whom God showed Himself glorious.

Acts 10:34-36 *"Peter fairly exploded with his good news: 'It's God's own truth, nothing could be plainer: God plays no favorites! It makes no difference who you are or where you're from—if you want God and are ready to do as He says, the door is open.'" **(MSG)***

Enjoy your journey as you walk through *Tabernacle Stories of Faith.*

Notes

[1] Taken from website, http://www.nyise.org/fanny/index.html, accessed 9/17/07

OUR HISTORY, OUR HERITAGE
at
TABERNACLE BAPTIST CHURCH

On September 30th of this year, 2007, Pastor Hattaway preached a sermon based on **Joshua 4** in which he said, **"We need to remember what God has done so that we can move forward to what He has called us YET to do."** He went on to tell of the hardships our founding fathers faced in 1911 as they fulfilled God's call to start a new church in Cartersville. It was no coincidence that the Friday prior to this service, as I was compiling this book, I had been "led" to visit our Tabernacle Heritage Room on the 2nd floor. As I looked at all the treasured keepsakes of our church's history, read articles and looked at pictures of "days gone by," I realized that God was speaking. He was reminding me, through these photographs and articles, that the ministry and beauty we enjoy today at Tabernacle were the fruit of someone else's labor – someone else's sacrifice and dedication. A church does not just "spring up." It must be nurtured, watered and cared for by those who have vision.

Our forefathers had vision – vision for this community and vision for this church. Our pastor and staff have that same vision. So should we. **Proverbs 29:19** says, *"Where there is no **vision**, the **people** perish."* (emphasis added) Vision is the key to progress and to fulfilling God's call. By looking back, let us gain resolve to move forward. May the lives and sacrifices of the generations before us never be wasted on our watch. May we be found faithful as we carry out God's vision through God's work in THIS generation.

In October of 1925, a precious member of Tabernacle, Miss Minnie Spence, wrote down the history of our church. The following is an excerpt from her article.

> "About 15 years ago, (1911), God, through the Holy Spirit, came into the heart of an humble servant living about five miles from Cartersville, with so strong an appeal that he, George F. Brown, should begin a work on the east side of Cartersville. Things looked dark and gloomy for this humble servant of His. To undertake the organization of a church, with practically no foundation, no home, no organized body, was a task that could not be accomplished by a man. For about eight months this man of God cherished in his

heart the call of God to establish a church in East Cartersville. After talking with several of Christ's disciples about this call, the day was fixed for the organization of the Baptist Church. Permission was secured to use the Presbyterian Church on Tennessee Street.

On the 26th of March, 1911, a small congregation assembled in this old church for the purpose of organizing a Baptist Church. From man's view, the outlook seemed discouraging, for the day was cold and rainy and the crowd small. Gathered around the heater, these followers of Christ, 15 in number, bringing letters from other Baptist churches, bound themselves together to be a light on the east side of Cartersville, witnessing for Him who had bought them with His own precious blood."

Can you imagine that cold rainy day in 1911? Everyone present had to walk or ride in a horse and buggy! Yet they did not let gloomy circumstances and bad weather deter them. How hard this is for us to imagine from the comfort of our padded pews! Aren't we thankful for these precious founders?! This faithful ban of 15 followers stepped out in faith, determined to fulfill the call God had placed on their lives to start a fresh work in Cartersville – to shine Christ's light for others to see. May we be no less determined to fulfill the call of God on each of **our** lives and the corporate work He has called us to at Tabernacle.

Continuing with Miss Minnie Spence's history:

"These 15 people, Mr. and Mrs. J.G. Smith, Mr. and Mrs. C.E. Smith, Gertie and Lona Smith, Buford Smith, Mr. and Mrs. Lonnie Smith, Mr. G.O. Smith, Mr. nd Mrs. W.L. Blair, daughter Rebecca Blair, Mr. Luther Ingram, and Mrs. Sara Holland, held conference the following Sunday, April 2nd, and called as their pastor, Rev. George F. Brown.

It was in April that the pastor held his first protracted service . . . four additions were made to the church. It was in the same month, the 19th day, that the Church, in conference, named the church, "East Side Baptist." The Sunday School was organized . . . the officers and teachers were chosen as wisely as possible. The number of pupils enrolled was 275. The path was long and difficult.

In May 1911, a committee was appointed to purchase the building, that the church might have a house in which to worship. The building was bought from the Presbyterians for the sum of $500. Learning later that the lot on which the church was built did not go with the building, in March 1912 the church bought the ground on which the building stood.

The first of September, 1911, delegates were sent to the Middle Cherokee Association to apply for membership. In this same month a meeting was held and 81 additions were made to the Church, 39 having come by baptism. Records show that the church had increased to a membership of 106 at this time. **The abiding spirit and the growth of the church was enough in itself to convince one that the Lord had planted this church here. God works in mysterious ways, and is anxious to use each life for the progress of His Kingdom."**

In October of 1953, after the death of Miss Minnie Spence in 1950, Mrs. W.R. McDaniel was asked to continue the chronicle of the Church's history. The following paragraph is taken from her article.

"During Rev. Crowe's pastorate (1924-1944) the church membership increased to nearly 1100 members. At the close of one revival in 1932, he baptized in one afternoon (at Pettit's Creek), 164 into the Church, and another time, in August of 1936, he baptized 109 in one afternoon. In some cases, members of entire families were baptized at the same time."

What must it have been like in 1932 or 1936 when the Holy Spirit brought Revival upon Tabernacle, bringing entire families to repentance and saving faith in Jesus Christ? May we see this same outpouring in our generation! **Joel 2:28** *"And it shall come to pass afterward, that I will **pour out my spirit** upon* *all flesh; and your sons and your daughters shall prophesy, your old men shall dream dreams, your young men shall see visions"(emphasis added).*

When the foundation of our church was being poured, a Bible was placed beneath the pulpit. The work that God has done here is figuratively and literally built on His Word! We are told in **Philippians 1:6** that God finishes what He starts, *"being confident of this, that he who began a good work in you will carry it on to completion until the day of Christ Jesus."* When God started His work at East Side Baptist Church (Tabernacle) in 1911, He had a completed work in mind, not a partial job. What is left to be done? What is God's heart and vision for Tabernacle in this generation and beyond? Let us pursue that vision together in one accord, being of "like mind and like heart."

***Ephesians 2:20** (emphasis added): "**Together, we are his house, built on the foundation of the apostles and the prophets. And the cornerstone is Christ Jesus himself!**"*

GOD'S PROVISION
by
Nick Adams

"He will call upon me, and I will answer him; I will be with him in trouble, I will deliver him and honor him."
Psalm 91:15

Several years ago a Sunday school class member's, (Margaret Ivey), car blew up on I-75 one morning going to work in Atlanta. Being a single mother of 2 children, she could not afford another car. Margaret shared this situation with our class and we made it a priority for that week to pray for a car. The very next week, I got a call from our best friends, Barbara and Mitch Mitchell. They had a car which belonged to their daughter who had gotten married the year before. They were tired of it just sitting there in the driveway being an eyesore in their neighborhood. They wanted to know if we knew of anyone needing a car. Of course, we said yes, and told them about Margaret's situation.

Since the car needed some repairs before it could be driven, we put the word out in our class. Again, things started happening. We rented a tow truck and Danny Rampley, a class member, towed it to his place. He checked it out, and found all the things that needed to be fixed. Debbie Everett, another class member, was working for a car dealership and she made some calls. We got a new muffler, new tires, battery, and brake job all done at no cost. For the next four years she drove that car and every time any of the class members saw it parked in the church parking lot we would lay hands on it and ask God to bless it. God is good!

Last year Chris Collins, a single mom working two jobs, got hit by a person who ran a red light. Unfortunately, Chris's car was totaled. The money she got from her insurance was not enough to buy a decent car. Again, the class started praying for a car for Chris. A few weeks later, the same friend, Barbara Mitchell, called us. Her husband, Mitch, had died a few weeks prior to this and she wanted to give his old car to someone who needed it. I bought the car for $200 and gave it to Chris to drive until she could find one she could afford. Patrick Brooks, a class member that owns a salvage place, gave us a much needed muffler and it was ready to go. Again, God provided! What are you trusting Him to provide for you?

GOD IS SUFFICIENT
by
LISA BAGNELL

"And the peace of God, which transcends all understanding, will guard your hearts and your minds in Christ Jesus."
Philippians 4:7

I grew up in a good Christian home with solid values and lots of love. I was saved when I was nine, but I really didn't begin to grasp what it meant to have Jesus as Lord of my life until I was about 14. Through all of my growing up years, faith was easy for me. Life had never really been hard, so it was easy to believe that God loved me and always did what was best for me. Sure, there were times when I went my own way, but I never doubted God's presence or His love for me.

There have been many faith-building experiences over the course of my adult life, but none more difficult than what we have experienced over the last few years. You see, as a young married couple, my husband Mark and I struggled with typical young married things, money, kids, time together, but we always had our families to help us through. At 31 years of age, although we had lost extended members of our families and friends, neither of us had experienced the loss of anyone close to us. We had six grandparents between us. Mark's dad's parents died when Mark was very young and he had little memory of them. We had always said that we knew we had been blessed to have them for so long, but we had no idea what was in store for us. It was to be a time of great growth for our entire family.

It all began one July day in 2001. We had just returned from a week at the beach with my parents, grandparents, and my brother's family. That night on the news we heard the tragic story of a Georgia family that had been involved in a fatal accident in Texas. It wasn't until the next day that we learned that one of the people in that car was our 15 year-old special needs nephew. He lived with a caretaker in Marietta. Unbeknown to his parents, the caretaker, along with his mother and a friend, had taken Chase with him to pick up his nieces and nephews in Texas and bring them back to Georgia for the summer. The van they were riding in flipped over the side of a bridge and into a river killing five of the seven people inside. Chase had been securely strapped in the back seat of the van and was killed in the accident.

As the family was still reeling from this incident, Mark's mother, Marianna, was diagnosed with a malignant melanoma on the back of her leg in August. She had surgery in September and doctors felt that they were able to remove all of the cancer and that she would not need further treatment. They did tell her that melanoma can reoccur at any time and that she needed to keep a close eye out for any changes. Also in September, Mark's grandfather (Poppy) in Virginia was diagnosed with terminal lung cancer. Doctors really did not expect him to make it more than a few months and he seemed to be fading quickly. Over the next few weeks all of the children, grandchildren, and many of the great-grandchildren were able to make the trip to Virginia to visit with him. We went the second week in October. Poppy was very weak and mostly unaware of our visit, but we had a fabulous visit with Memaw (Mark's grandmother). We were shocked when just two weeks later on Halloween we got the call that Memaw had suffered a ruptured aorta and had died. We made the trip to Virginia knowing that another trip for another funeral would follow in the not too distant future.

In December of 2001 my dad, who had always been the picture of health, began to show some symptoms of prostate problems. He underwent a biopsy and in January of 2002 was diagnosed with metastasized prostate cancer. His PSA, which a normal count is below two and above four is very high, was in the 220s. Doctors told him to get his affairs in order because he was going to die. Dad's cancer in some ways turned out to be a real blessing. If you had told me before he was diagnosed what was going to happen, I would have told you that dad would sit in his chair, be grumpy, and die. But God got a hold of him and his whole life changed. He was always happy, always positive, and always telling people how good God is. He began treatments and his body responded miraculously. There was a time when the doctors just shook their heads in amazement. People would ask Dad how he was and he would say, "I'm wonderful!" – and he meant it! He felt better and had a better outlook on life than he had ever had. It was truly a testament to God's goodness.

In March of 2002 Poppy succumbed to the lung cancer. In May of that same year my grandmother, who had been suffering with Alzheimer's for many years, also passed away. At this point dad was doing well and Marianna was showing no signs of cancer at all. For about two years we were able to go on knowing and understanding that all things happen for a reason and that God was working out His perfect plan.

In the spring of 2004, Marianna, Mark's mother, found another spot on the same leg just a few inches higher than the first spot. She went in for a biopsy and was told that the cancer had returned. We all assumed that the process would be the same as before, have surgery to remove the cancer, some tissue around it and a few lymph nodes, but that was not to be. By the time she went in to have the surgery she had several lumps under the skin all over her body. Originally we were told that the cancer had spread and she had 18 – 24 months to live, but within a few short weeks we were down to 4-6 months with treatment. The cancer had spread to her lungs and her brain and it was all over her body. We prayed diligently for her healing, but knew that our time with her was short.

Over that same summer, dad began to experience some more symptoms that indicated his cancer was spreading also. He started having days when he didn't feel "wonderful" anymore. As we went into the fall, we struggled to make memories we could hold on to forever. Marianna made the decision to cease treatment because she felt so bad that she couldn't enjoy the life she had left. Dad spent a lot of time in the hospital and going back and forth to different treatments. The tumors in his lymph system had caused his legs to swell to a point where he couldn't move them to drive and walking was very difficult for him.

In November my grandmother (dad's mom) was diagnosed with breast cancer and had surgery to remove the cancer. A week after her surgery my grandfather, her husband, fell down a flight of stairs at their house. He broke his neck in the fall. He lived for almost a week in intensive care, but in the end he succumbed to the injuries that he had sustained. Mom told me later that just a few weeks prior to his fall, he was leaving from visiting Dad one day and when he hugged her he told her that they had to get Dad better because he couldn't bury his son. Dad was an only child and Papa just didn't think he could face that.

In December Marianna made a marked turn. She went from being active and mentally with it, to being house bound and mentally very far away. As she and Dad both worsened drastically over this time I often wondered if they were racing to heaven, trying to see who could get there first. Marianna won the race on February 2, 2005. She passed away peacefully with her children gathered around her. We were able to feel God's grace being poured out on us. Once again, I was assured of God's love and goodness for us.

As winter turned to spring and spring to summer, Dad's condition worsened with every day. Mom had to take a leave of absence from work in April because Dad could no longer do anything for himself. I prayed that God would allow me to finish the school year so that I could spend time with dad before he died. God granted that prayer. Dad spent most of June in the hospital fighting infections. Mom and I talked often about knowing that dad was dying, but it was not a conversation Dad was ready to have yet.

One morning in July, after talking with his doctor on the phone, Dad told mom that he was ready for Hospice and he laid out his funeral arrangements along with everything he wanted done. Over the course of a few hours he shared with Mom all of the things he wanted her to do and answered all of the questions that she had been pondering without her having to ask a single one. Hospice came in that day. We did not expect dad to make it very long. He had already been without food and water for almost a week when Hospice was called in, but he had also been on IVs that had caused his body to swell because it was unable to process the fluids.

The nurses told us what we could watch for as the end neared. They had to give the worst case scenario because it is part of their job, but I was sure that God would not allow that to happen with Dad. In all of the other experiences that we had been through, God had taken away pain and suffering and I expected nothing less for Dad. Unfortunately God had other plans. Because of the location of the worst of Dad's tumors the worst case scenario was that his intestines would be blocked by the tumors, eventually rupturing. We were told that should this happen it would be the most excruciating pain for several hours, and that it would end in death.

As the weeks wore on, this impossible scenario became more and more real. I prayed desperately by Dad's bedside for God to take him home. Dad was miserable but he never complained. He was in a great deal of pain. The cancer had attacked his bones and even the smallest movement was painful. He became unable to communicate with us verbally, but would sit and look at us as we talked to him. I really think he had a couple of personal goals that he wanted to reach despite the pain. On August 2nd he celebrated his 40th anniversary with the only company that he ever worked for. On August 7th he and mom celebrated their 40th wedding anniversary. They were supposed to be on the beach in Hawaii celebrating their anniversary and his retirement, but instead we were watching him slip away from us.

On August the 8th we knew that what we had prayed not to happen was going to happen. All of the signs we had been told we would see in case of an intestinal rupture began to appear. Dad was in agony. The physical side-effects were unbearable for us, but nothing compared to what Dad had to endure. All through the night mom and I sat by his side giving him a dropper full of liquid morphine every 5 minutes. He was getting massive amounts of morphine through a pump every 10 minutes and still he laid there and moaned with every breath. I have to be honest and say that I was mad at God those last few days. I had begged and pleaded with Him to allow Dad to die peacefully. I felt like God had abandoned us in our hour of greatest need. I couldn't believe that a God who said He loves us would allow Dad to suffer so much. It got to a point where I stopped asking for God to intervene and stopped talking to Him. If He was going to ignore me then I was going to ignore Him. Around 7:45 in the morning on August 9th, Dad began to calm down. Around 8:00 his breathing began to slow. Mom, my brother Larry, and I were watching the news coverage of the space shuttle landing. It was the first one since the fatal accident a few years ago. At 8:12, as the space shuttle touched down, dad breathed his last breath. In that instant the thought went through my head, "Now I understand the song *It Is Well with My Soul*." A peace like I had never known flooded my being and I knew that God was there and that He had been there all along. I still to this day don't understand why Dad had to suffer so, but I learned about a whole new aspect of God's love that I had never understood before. I understood about the peace that passes all understanding for the first time in my life. You see in all that we had been through before, God acted when I expected Him to. No, the outcome wasn't always what I asked for, but I could see God's hand. This time I had to learn how to trust His heart.

Since Dad's death we have lost two more people, my grandfather and a great-aunt who was like a grandmother to me. Mark and I have buried nine immediate family members in the last five years. Through it all I have learned that God is sufficient. I have learned that God's plans are not my own. I've learned that I can go on because God is alive and working every minute of every day – even when I can't see it. My faith is nowhere near perfect, but for Chase, Memaw, Poppy, Nana, Papa, Marianna, Dad, Papa, and Aunt Louise, their faith has been made sight! Because of their lives and their deaths, my faith and the faith of many who knew them has been strengthened.

A TESTIMONY TO GOD'S FAITHFULNESS
by
LISA BANDY

"But be sure to fear the LORD and serve him faithfully with all your heart; consider what great things he has done for you."
I Samuel 12:24

My life is a story of God's faithfulness. Even as a young child, I had a desire to be with God's people and live for Him. I was very involved in my home church and took every opportunity to participate, lead, and volunteer. Through the years, God continued to work in my life, and as a junior in high school, I felt led to dedicate my life to full-time Christian service, not knowing exactly where that would lead. In college I majored in elementary education, but didn't feel that being a school teacher was exactly what God had for me. After college graduation, I felt that I should go to seminary. This was a definite step of faith, since my parents weren't in favor of it, and I wasn't sure how I would make it financially. Predictably, God met my needs through support of my home church, friends at seminary, and a job on campus.

After seminary, God continued to surprise me in His leading. I left seminary to take a position as Director of Student Development at Shorter College, something I never would have dreamed would have been part of my life. Working with college students, especially since I was just slightly older than they were, was a challenge and a delight. God, of course, continued to work "all things together for good" **(Rom. 8:28)** in my life. I worked with some great people, and became involved in a church with friends who had a tremendous influence on my life. During my last year at Shorter, I met Tom, who was on staff at Tabernacle at that time, and life took another direction as we married, and God opened new opportunities. I shifted to the other end of the educational spectrum, and started teaching preschoolers.

After a couple of years, we left Tabernacle, and while our girls were young, were involved in a small church where we volunteered in many areas. This gave me the opportunity to be a full-time Mom, which was another "desire of my heart" **(Ps. 37:4)** that God met. Later I served that church in a part-time position working with the preschool and children's ministries.

As our girls reached teenage years, we felt that we needed to move to a church where they could have a greater opportunity to be challenged in their faith and walk. Again, God was at work in His timing and purpose. We visited Tabernacle and felt this was the place for our family. I remember thinking on one of our first visits that I couldn't imagine being responsible for such a large number of children (I know God was chuckling as He knew what was ahead for me). Soon the opportunity was presented for me to come on staff here as interim in the children's ministry – and the rest is almost five more years of His working His plan in our lives as a family.

God is so faithful to His word and promises! Looking back confirms that He is in control. He has "worked things together for good" and has given me "the desires of my heart" over and over, not always as I have asked or expected, but always above and beyond what I could imagine. A life blessed by Him, a husband who loves the Lord more than life itself, and daughters who have hearts for the Lord are all a testimony of His work and His goodness.

BLESSED ASSURANCE
by
GAYLE BECK

*"But as for me, I will sing about your power. Each morning I will sing with joy about your unfailing love. For you have been my refuge, a place of safety when I am in distress.
O my Strength, to you I sing praises, for you, O God, are my refuge,
the God who shows me unfailing love."
Psalms 59:16-17 (MSG)*

On October 20, 1996 at the "young age" of 41, I accepted Christ as my Savior. There were no flashes of light or great visions from above. There **was** a wonderful sense of peace and assurance. Several days before, a fellow choir member, Mike LaRue, had accepted Christ during choir practice. Then, the following Sunday morning, October 20, he shared with the congregation how he had been living with doubts concerning his salvation. He decided on that Wednesday night to "nail it down". As Mike was sharing his testimony, I could totally relate! For you see, as a small child, I had "walked the aisle" with my Dad and we were both baptized. As a teenager, I was very active with my youth group at church. I was in church every Sunday and Wednesday, sang in the youth choir and went on mission trips. It was during my teenage years that I began to experience doubts concerning my salvation. Those doubts would plague me for many years and I would "rededicate" my life. But, I never truly felt the sense of peace and assurance I was so desperately seeking.

So, as Mike was sharing his testimony, I realized that I did not want to go another minute with these doubts. I now understood in my heart that Christ did not want me living with doubts and fears. He wanted a personal relationship with me that was full of love, assurance and acceptance.

Now, Mike was giving his testimony before the pastor had a chance to give his sermon and ask for an altar call. When Mike finished, he just asked that if anyone was living with doubts, they could settle it right then and there. I knew there was no way I wanted to spend another minute without His assurance. So, I decided not to waste another second. I went down before the sermon OR the altar call! Others came as well – my sweet friend Gail Warren and my son, Brent. What a glorious day!

Like I said, no flashes of light – just wonderful, heavenly assurance. It's like the words of the old hymn, "Blessed Assurance." …"Blessed Assurance, Jesus is mine. Oh what a foretaste of Glory divine."

Years have passed and I can honestly say that I have not doubted my salvation. Not even for a moment. Was my salvation experience as a young child real or not? I have been asked that question on several occasions. My response is always the same. It no longer matters. What **does** matter is that on October 20, 1996 my salvation was "nailed down". It is no longer important to me whether it was the "real thing" as a small child. What truly matters is that Jesus is real to me now! He is my Savior and Lord! He is my Rock and Foundation. He is my source of strength.

I wish I could say that since October 20, 1996 my life has been easy and perfect, but I can't. Life is full of trials and hurt, physical and emotional pain, loss of precious friends and family, and tough decisions that sometimes have to be made. And because I am a sinner, many mistakes have been made. But, oh how blessed I am to have a Savior to see me through. A mighty Rock to lean on! How grateful I am for His strength when I am weak. How awed I am at His bountiful mercy and grace He shows me when I am unworthy. His love never fails me.

I have learned that life is precious and very short. I would encourage others to **please not let another minute go by without the total assurance of being saved by His grace!** We are all sinners and all we have to do is admit this and ask Him into our hearts – to come and have a relationship with us. It is truly just that easy.

SAVED BY FAITH
by
DARLENE BENTON

"For it is by grace you have been saved, through faith—and this not from yourselves, it is the gift of God"
Ephesians 2:8

I grew up in a small Baptist church in Blue Ridge, Ga. Church was the focal point of our family life. We were there just about anytime the doors were open and Daddy (who accepted Christ in his 60's) made sure we were on time, which was always no less than 30 minutes before the service was to begin. I was involved in church in the choir, singing groups (can't sing but I stood in the gap for someone), playing the piano, etc. Even with this, I went through a long period of recurring doubt about my salvation. After all, I didn't have a testimony that Jesus saved me from a life of drugs, drinking or a life of crime like some. No lightening bolt experience here!

Some years later I was visiting Mother (Daddy had gone home to Jesus by now), and as I sat in the living room the doubts came flooding in. I said in my spirit, "God, if I haven't said or been sincere enough, I want to say it now, please give me peace and take this doubt away."

God through his Word has taught me that we don't have to have lived a sin-filled life in order to have a testimony. He saved me <u>from</u> making those mistakes. Praise God!

Know this, we aren't saved based on our feelings but based on faith in God's Word.

What a future we have in Christ. I am excited about what is yet to be! See you there!

FEAR NOT
by
ED BRUCE

"What time I am afraid I will trust in Thee."
Psalms 56:3(KJV)

Years ago when our children were young, our youngest son was having trouble going to sleep at night. In an effort to comfort him, my wife wrote this verse on a small piece of paper and taped it to the wall beside his bed. She assured him that God would take care of him through the night.

I often thought that this was very wise of her to use God's Word to comfort a child. I did not realize how comforting God's Word could be to an adult. However, on Friday, November 5th, 2005 I came to realize that as an adult, I needed the comfort of these words also.

After experiencing chest pains in the middle of the night and being treated at the local hospital I was transported to Redmond Hospital in Rome, Georgia to have a catheterization test for a possible blockage. The test revealed that I had seven blockages. Three would need to be bypassed and four would need to be treated with a Laser. When I awoke and was advised of my condition, I found out what it was like to be afraid. I had experienced many trials in my 65 years but never anything like this.

As I waited for the surgery, I had many thoughts about unfinished projects, and unspoken words to family and friends. As my family, ministers, and doctors visited with me, I realized more than ever that God's Word is a comfort for all, for adults **and** children, and "What time I am Afraid I will trust in God."

Now as I approach two years since my heart surgery, I can truly say to all, "**WHAT TIME YOU ARE AFRAID YOU CAN TRUST IN GOD!**"

WINGS OF GOD
by
JUDY BRUCE

*How precious is your loving kindness, oh Lord God,
therefore the children of men put their trust under
the shadow of your wings.
Psalms 36:7 (KJV)*

As I think back over the years of my life, there are certain times that I remember God doing a specific thing to meet a specific need. God has never failed me when I needed Him nor left me alone to take care of myself. He has always been there for me on the mountain tops of my life and what seemed to be the deepest, darkest valleys!

All of us have mountaintop and valley experiences but more often, we live the days, weeks, months and years given to us on a steady even path. Sometimes, very unexpectedly though, we find ourselves in that valley and there seems to be no way out. Because we think there is no way out……..we look up.

In what seems to be a long-ago summer of my life, I was told I needed a very serious surgery. Laying in that cold sterile operating room, surrounded by doctors and nurses, I felt alone but I knew I was not alone. I had prayed that God would let me hear the flutter of angel's wings around me and I would be comforted because I knew He was near. I did not hear angel wings, but for that moment in time, so many years ago, I looked up and saw a beautiful monarch butterfly, hovering right above my face, so close I could feel the air stirred by it's wings. My heart filled with joy because God had reached out to me from heaven. I watched that butterfly for only a few seconds and as I raised my hand to touch him …..he was gone.

I felt that wonderful peace one feels when they know that God has heard and answered their prayer. I was not alone and God was there. Amy Carmichael said: "If God can make his birds to whistle in drenched and stormy darkness, if He can make his butterflies able to bear up under rain, what can He not do for the heart that trusts in Him?" That golden butterfly has been a constant reminder in all the circumstances of my life that there is no better place to put my trust than under the shadow of God's wings.

GOD IS FAITHFUL THROUGH THE YEARS
by
LOUISE DEE
(WRITTEN BY CATHY PARKER)

"Thou wilt keep him in perfect peace, whose mind is stayed on Thee because he trusteth in Thee."
Isaiah 26:3 (KJV)

March 1, 2007 will mark 80 years that God in His mercy has allowed me to live on this earth. Much has transpired since I was born including God's grace and miracles, but with God's help I will attempt to record a small part of my story.

In May 1946, for the first time, peace came into my heart at the church altar. This marked the beginning of a new life. At the time, I was enrolled in nursing school, the director of nurses had a massive heart attack. Subsequently the school closed due to lack of professional help during the war. To have remained in that environment would have been difficult to serve God. My pastor suggested I join the church's young people in attending a Bible Camp in Massachusetts. In an evening of Evangelistic Service I dedicated my life to the Lord and promised to serve him wherever He would lead.

On the next day, which was the 4th of July, I met the camp nurse. We discussed my nursing school closing. I was also introduced to a nurse superintendent of a near by hospital. She invited me to visit the nursing school on my way home. In so many ways God was guiding each day. Six of my former classmates and I transferred to the nursing school in Greater Boston where I graduated.

While I was attending school in Greater Boston, I attended a Missionary Convention. Another battle came my way. Was I willing to serve the Lord in caring for Lepers in Vietnam? Often times God only wants us willing — I only cared for one Leper, a precious soul who also had T.B.

After graduating, I returned home to work in a local hospital. My pastor questioned me as to my call to the mission field. I felt God would open the door. The pastor convinced me to apply to missionary college, even though the classes were full. A miracle came and I was accepted. I was on my way to missionary school.

After graduating, I was appointed to a Leprosarium in Vietnam only to get that door closed because of the war. Another door opened in the fall of 1956 to serve the Lord in a hospital in Pakistan. I was to sail, but only to encounter more hindrances including a dock strike, which held our sailing for a month. At last my co-missionary and I were part of nine people on a freighter ship. As we were nearing the Suez Canal our captain was pacing the deck above. There had been rumors of the bombing of the canal. Our ship was the last convoy to go through the canal before it was bombed. God was gracious to us again. We reached Karachi unharmed. We made it through customs and finally we were on our way to ride the train to Multan. Our compartment on the train was packed with women, children and luggage. The men rode in a separate train car. The long dusty train trip was slowly coming to an end. As we stared out the window, there was dear Marion (Senior Missionary) holding flowered leis and waving. Soon we were packed into a horse drawn carriage. We were on our way to what would be our home for the next five years.

Our hospital had a Midwifery College and only treated women and children. The men could gather in a Bible room while they waited to hear from their wives. All the patients were Muslim women who kept Purda (Veiled). They always had to wear a veil to cover their faces in public and around other men. After arriving, we started language studies and attending Nightar Midwifery College, as we had not had Midwifery yet in the states. All of our delivery cases were taken in our hospital as we had plenty of patients. One of my patients, arriving very late and very pregnant with three babies, was ready to be delivered. Dr. K allowed me to deliver the babies with her in the room. The mother had a lot of toxicity in her body and the triplet babies did not survive.

After passing my midwifery exams, my mornings consisted of attempting to take histories of the incoming patients. The written language of Pakistan is Urdu. Most of our students came in from Punjabi area. Our patients lived mostly in Multan or the surrounding areas. In order to take histories oftentimes you had to speak through three different interpreters.

I learned early on to depend on the Lord in making decisions which confronted me. A dear little girl put a baby in my arms and told me the baby was mine. I told the little girl that I would return immediately and to wait there. I went to confer with Dr. K. When I returned the girl and baby were gone. With the help of some interpreters, they said a woman had offered the girl a few rupees and the little girl gave her the baby. I was told the baby would probably grow up to be a slave. We kept orphans until we could find them a Christian family and home.

Although my furlough was due, I was allowed to stay another year so our Senior Missionary could take an anesthesia course in the States and our nursing students could take their exams in Multan. It became difficult for me to sit at the table and eat because of weakness. Through tests, we learned that our cook had TB and I had contracted it. At first the cable came for me to fly home immediately and the tickets were being sent. In my devotions that morning, I read in Isaiah, *"Ye shall not go out in haste or in flight."* My co-missionary and future travel companion came in to assure me everything was packed and ready for the train to Karachi. I had just felt assurance from the Lord that this was not to be, so I told my missionary companion that I had heard from the Lord and we would not be traveling today. Before noon, another cable came from New York saying plans had changed and that my medicine was being flown out and I was to remain for a period of time. The doctor from the clinic in Muntarabad came to take me to their quarters at the clinic. They felt I would not get any rest with the students coming to my room. After returning to the hospital in Karachi, I was preparing to leave on the train to Karachi and once again difficulties had arisen. My temperature had gone up and malaria had attacked again. Having felt the Lord had healed me from TB, this was another let down.

One of the doctors from another mission hospital came to visit me and she knew a new medicine for malaria that had not yet been patented, but said she was able to get it if I was willing to take it and that they have had good results from it. I praised the Lord and I told her I would be willing to take it. They brought me two vials and I only took one and immediately my temperature was back to normal. I carried the other vial across the ocean with me. I was able to get up and board the ship that took us home.

When I arrived in the United States, my father and brother in-law met me at the docks. I was unable to go home with them because I had to make several visits in New York to Dr. Franes. He said for me not to return to his office for two years. By that time I was married and expecting my first child.

There have been many tests and trials but along with blessings. God has been so merciful in granting me such a full life. Seven great-grand children and Dean and Cathy are expecting a little boy named Zachary in June which will make eight. All are so special. I am so thankful for the promise *"You shall be saved and your house hold."*

I remember a Bible school student said to me, "Louise you are just too negative." What had happened to my *"Count it all joy"*? *(James 1:2)* But through the years, He is still my Savior, Sanctifier and Healer, Glorious Lord, and Coming King.

TOUCHED BY AN ANGEL
by
ANNE DONAHOO

"An angel from heaven appeared to him and strengthened him."
Luke 22:43

God has been at work in my life for all of my life – as far back as I can remember. But there is one thing He did which I will never forget and I want to relay that story to you.

It was 1996 and I had taken a trip to Helen, Georgia by myself. I had done this for many years around the same time just to be alone with God and spend time in prayer and the Word. I remember that I was reading R. A. Torey's book, *The Power of Prayer* and it had really spoken to me.

I left my condo to run a few errands and had returned later on, planning to spend a quiet evening in prayer and reading. As the night went on, I began to wheeze. I called my husband, Brother, to let him know that I was not feeling well and that I would drive home early the next morning. He was very concerned. After insisting that he would drive up immediately, I begged him not to because it was a long drive and it was getting so late. I assured him I would go to bed early and be home first thing in the morning.

After going to bed, I awoke around midnight to find my body almost completely immobile. It took all the strength I had to make it to the phone and call Brother. I told him I was calling 911 and that I would call him when we got to the hospital. (I did not know where they would take me.)

I immediately hung up and dialed 911. I told the operator where I was and what was happening to me, but did not give her my name. She asked me if I could make it to the front door to unlock it. I told her I would try. She stayed on the line as I laid down the phone and struggled to make it to the door.

About the time I got there, I heard a voice on the other side say, "Mrs. Donahoo, I am a police officer. May I come in?" I was amazed that he knew my name. But that thought quickly left me as I let him in.

He was wonderfully kind and began asking me questions and trying to get my mind off of my physical condition. We talked about many things. I eventually told him about my wonderful Sunday School class at Tabernacle and how much they all meant to me. He told me a few things about himself and that his name was Eric, but mostly he comforted me.

It finally occurred to me that I had left the 911 operator on hold. I got the phone and told her there was a nice police officer waiting with me. Sounding puzzled, she replied, "There is a police officer **there** with you **now**?" She went on to say that she was dispatching an ambulance and it would be there right away. Then I hung up.

Within a few minutes, the ambulance arrived. As they came in the door with the gurney, the policeman leaned over me, kissed me on the forehead and placed an angel pin in my hand. He said, "Just remember, this is your guardian angel."

As the medics were placing me in the back of the ambulance, I thought it strange that they were parked in the same parking space, just outside my condo door, that the police officer had been in. How could they have parked in the same place at the same time?

The next thing I knew, I was in the back of the ambulance being rushed to the hospital. After a few minutes, I asked the medic if he knew that policeman who had stayed with me. He looked very puzzled and he said, "Mrs. Donahoo, there was no one with you when we arrived. You were alone in the condo." I held out my hand to show him the angel pin. "Look", I said, "He was there. He gave me this." The medic was looking at me like I had hallucinated or dreamed it all. I knew that I hadn't.

After settling in to the emergency room, the nurse approached my bed and asked me to tell her about the officer who had waited with me. So, I told her exactly what had happened, gave her a description of him and told her his name was Eric.

I will never forget her words to me. She looked me straight in the eye and said, "Mrs. Donahoo, I have lived in Helen all of my life. I know everyone here. Not only that, but I live right next door to the police station. There is **not** a police officer in Helen who fits that description **or** who is named Eric!" When the doctor arrived, the nurse asked me to relay my story to him as well. I did. He listened intently, then asked me, "Do you think it could have been an angel?" I was speechless. It was becoming clear to me that God had sent an angel to care for me!

That same day, it was confirmed by my doctor, Dr. Mason Brown, that I indeed had suffered a stroke which had paralyzed the entire left side of my body.

I stayed in rehabilitation in Rome for a month and continued for another year and a half with outpatient therapy. I had to learn to walk all over again. It was a difficult time, but I never felt alone or afraid. I knew that God had been with me the entire time and I could feel the prayers of so many lifted up for me and for Brother during those days.

How I thank God for his amazing visitation to me! I have my angel pin in a safe place and I will tell my story as long as I have breath. I pray that as you read it, if you have struggled with belief in God or with trusting Him, that you will be challenged to believe that God is real and that He is who He says He is…a great and mighty God who deserves our dedication, worship and praise!

BEAUTY FOR ASHES
by
BETTY MERCER FAILE

*"To bestow on them a crown of **beauty** instead of **ashes**, the oil of gladness instead of mourning, and a garment of praise instead of a spirit of despair. They will be called oaks of righteousness, a planting of the LORD for the display of his splendor."*
Isaiah 61:3 (emphasis added)

Being the age of eight or nine years old, every afternoon when I came home from school I was to awaken my mother for her nurses job (afternoon to midnight shift). My Mother, Grandmother, and "Auntie" Blanche Lively were the three main nurses of Dr. Lester Harbin (of Harbin Clinic) in Rome, Georgia and of McCall Hospital.

Aside from her full time nursing shift, my mother was 911 before 911 began. She would often be called in emergency situations of neighbors, relatives and friends. A quick example is once when I went with my mother to aid a neighbor who had fallen in front of her front door while having some sort of attack. She was able to call my mother by phone before becoming totally unconscious. My mother used me by pushing me through an unlocked window. I pulled the lady's body from the doorway and let my mom in through the front door to help. Mrs. Jones had fallen from a heart attack. My mother immediately began CPR and pulled some medicines from her black bag. She stayed with Mrs. Jones until the ambulance arrived. Mrs. Jones survived and lived until a ripe old age.

Not only did my mom work as a nurse and local emergency contact, she was also a hospice nurse. She sat with cancer patients and tried to keep them as comfortable as possible. She used this time to minister to them spiritually as well. By the age of nine, I had seen at least six people draw their last breath; death was just a part of life to me. But it was one warm June day, nearing the end of the school year, when death hit closest to home for me.

I came home and went in to wake my mother for work as I always did. She did NOT wake up. An unforeseen aneurysm had exploded in her brain during the night. An unexplainable peace came over me as I dialed the hospital to tell them mother would not be in and to request an ambulance to my own house. I knew enough to check her for vital signs, but found none.

It was evident to me that she had passed away in the morning hours. I remember standing outside as the stretcher was placed in the back of the ambulance and the doors closed. What a turning point in my young life. How would I respond? I could choose to be angry and wonder why God had allowed this to happen to my mother at the young age of 42 when she was needed by so many.

Instead, a peace came over me, a gentle hug in the wind. I truly felt God's presence and love surround me. That day I found the meaning of the words "Consecrated to God". That day God became truly alive in my life and took over my parents' role and indeed became my Heavenly Father.

We've all seen the famous artwork of God's hand reaching down to man. That day, I felt God's hand come down from the sky and I heard Him call, "Child of mine".

The coming weeks and months were pretty tough for me and my 11-year-old sister. My father (13 years older than my mother) had been a prisoner of war in the Korean War. His captivity and the abuse he suffered left him with strong memories of wrath and bitterness in his heart. It didn't take long to see that he could not raise two daughters on his own. My mother's strength had held us together. He eventually retired to a Veteran's home where we visited him monthly until he passed away.

My sister and I lived in three different places during the year. During school months, we were under the guardianship of my father's sister who was a total atheist. But during the sweet summer months, we traveled to Hollywood, Florida and Savannah,

Georgia to live with my mother's sisters who were strong in the faith.

What a seesaw, rollercoaster life that started full speed at such a young age. It was apparent to me early on that we all make choices as to how we will live our lives, how we will handle situations, overcome hurt and bitterness, and let God take over when we have nothing else to give. It is ultimately our choice to submit to God or not. The necessity to secure your eternal salvation should not be put off, taken for granted or taken lightly. We never know what tomorrow may bring.

SAVED AND FORGIVEN
by
BERTHA FONTAINE

"And everyone who calls on the name of the Lord will be saved."
Acts 2:21

I learned the Ten Commandments, **Psalms 23, 100, and 121** in Sunday School as a child and was taught if I broke the commandments I'd go to hell.

My mother told us, "Jesus loves you." I knew Jesus' birthday was Christmas and that He died and rose again at Easter time, but I didn't know He did this for me, to pay for my sins.

When I was 27 years old, I got away from Jesus and the Bible verses I'd memorized. I realized I'd broken the Ten Commandments. God spoke to me really clear. "You're on your way to hell," He said. I was so afraid. I didn't want to live and I was afraid to die. I needed to find forgiveness for my sins. I prayed and prayed but knew God hadn't forgiven me. I didn't know Jesus as my Savior. I didn't know I needed to receive Him into my heart for God to forgive me.

We attended several different churches seeking forgiveness and didn't hear the Gospel. We saw painted on a huge rock, "Jesus Saves." We wondered what He saved.

When I was 41 years old, we attended a Southern Baptist church in Willimantic, Connecticut. The pastor said, "You don't have to go to hell for all those sins you're thinking about because Jesus died in your place and rose so you can have a new life." I was amazed. I knew God was speaking to me. Jesus saved me; God forgave me; and the Holy Spirit came to live within my heart.

A Testimony

When God convicted me so clear,
My heart and mind were filled with fear.
Please forgive me, Jesus, I prayed,
I was unhappy and afraid.

I didn't know why Jesus died,
Why Holy Spirit lives inside,
That Jesus rose, new life to give.
When I believed, God did forgive.

Now there is peace in heart and mind,
And I want always to be kind.
To meet all people with God's love,
And be with Him in heaven above.
Jesus died to set us all free,
Now I know what He did for me.
He paid the debt my sins incurred,
Are you listening? Have you heard?

We all sin and disobey,
We need forgiveness everyday.
I must confess when I do wrong.
God forgives, to Him I belong.

(Romans 3:23, 6:23, 5:8, I John 1:9, Ephesians 4:32)

-Bertha Fontaine

WHY CARTERSVILLE?
by
SHERRY GLAZE

A short chapter in the Glaze family story.

"And let us consider how we may spur one another on toward love and good deeds. Let us not give up meeting together, as some are in the habit of doing, but let us encourage one another—and all the more as you see the day approaching."
Hebrews 10:24-25

Words cannot begin to paint an accurate picture of the many ways God has chosen to bless the Glaze family. How could anyone have known that nine months prior to my birth in the small rural community near Poplar Bluff, Missouri my future spouse was beginning his life journey in Jasper, Alabama.

As God began to gently lay out the puzzle pieces, our lives slowly came closer and closer together. It is said that hindsight is always 20/20, but as you face the many ups and downs and changes of life, you're never quite sure why things are happening or how it is going to all fit together. With many differences, the foundations of both the Glaze and Smith families withstood some devastating events.

While serving the Lord and preparing to be the best pastor he could be, Gary's father was killed in a tragic car accident while attending New Orleans Baptist Seminary and serving as pastor in a small church in Santa Rosa, Mississippi. As Gary's mother struggled to raise two children, she continued to seek God's will for her life. Through the help of some very dear friends, God led her to the mountains of eastern Kentucky, where she attended school and later became the campus librarian at Clear Creek Baptist School in Pineville, Kentucky – a small preacher's college. It was in these mountains that Gary, along with his mother and sister were able to "mend."

After high school and two years of college at Eastern Kentucky University, Gary left the mountains of eastern Kentucky for the city streets of Birmingham, Michigan where his sister and brother-in-law were living. Uncertain as to what God had in store for him; Gary found work with one of the local industries and began attending Madison Heights Baptist Church where his sister attended.

During this same timeframe and several states away, God had been busy in the lives of the Smith family. With tough times falling on the small farming communities of southeastern Missouri, my dad sought work in the North and later sent for his little family. After moving north, my parents were instrumental in helping to establish a small, new mission where a relative served as the pastor and my dad served as the "Song Director" for many years. As this little church grew, the need for a larger facility became obvious. The church moved and became known as Madison Heights Baptist Church. I grew up in this church and attended Sunday School, Training Union, Sunbeams, and GAs. Unfortunately, by the time I reached my mid to late teens, church was not the center of my family's life. Regular attendance was not necessarily the norm. However, God's presence and teachings never left us. *"Train up a child in the way that he should go. Even when he is old he will not depart from it..."* **Proverbs 22:6**

It was at this time that Gary had begun attending this same church. Through the patient, "match making" attempts and persistence of a dear young friend, Gary and I finally met and began a friendship that changed our lives forever. We met in the fall of 1969, began dating in January 1970 and married in January 1971 and the rest is history...

Gary and I stayed in Michigan for a year and then returned to Eastern Kentucky University where he completed his degree in Industrial Arts, and I taught in Estill County. (I think I was more the student as I learned much from the children of Eastern Kentucky. It was quite a change for a "city girl." I grew up with sidewalks and streetlights. I had never seen such darkness at night.)

After graduation from EKU, Gary and I moved to a small town in western Kentucky where we made our home for the next 12 years. During that time we were blessed with three little girls – Amy, Rhonda, and Laura. Living away from family, our little church truly became our extended family. The girls grew up in a loving church where everyone knew and cared for each other.

One of our first family "crises" was when, at the age of two, Amy faced open heart surgery. Having no family close by, we leaned heavily on our church family for support and comfort during a very scary time.

Just about the time we thought we were "getting it altogether," the unexpected happened. A change in course offerings for the upcoming year led to the closing of the industrial arts department. Within one day's time we found out that Gary wouldn't have a teaching job the next year and the "ulcer" I thought I was developing was actually our third child, Laura. Surprise – surprise... (She always says that she knows God has something special planned for her – especially since she wasn't exactly planned.)

With a new child on the way, it wasn't really the best time for us to be looking for jobs elsewhere so we tried to stay put. I continued to teach and after trying to make a living by means of a small craft and picture framing business, Gary began working at the state penitentiary as the furniture plant supervisor. Now that was a unique experience. (Ask him about prison food sometime...)

Change is not usually easy. Picking up and moving your family is not something that is done without a lot of thought and planning. Even though we are always trying to listen and follow His guidance, we are often not very receptive to God's leading. Gary and I both believe that God was using this "in between" time to prepare us for our next move. We had to get uncomfortable.

As the girls grew, their love for Jesus grew also. We used to say that our three girls, their two best friends and a few others made up the entire children's department. They may have been small in number, but their enthusiasm and desire to learn more about Jesus was strong. Every Sunday School teacher, choir director, and GA leader played a critical role in their development as they helped them come to know Jesus a little better each week. While most children were playing house or ball, Amy and Rhonda were either teaching or preaching, and Laura usually got stuck being the student or the congregation.

Over the next two years as vocational education was changing in Kentucky, we realized that if Gary was going to get back into teaching, we might need to look at other states. Surviving a prison riot was also instrumental in helping us come to such a conclusion.

As we interviewed and were offered positions in other states and cities, Cartersville was the place that God laid on our hearts. It just seemed right. We had no family in Cartersville, no connections, nothing. We continued to pray about the direction for our family. As we interviewed – it seemed right. When our real estate agent, Doug Cochran, prayed with us in our hotel room about the right house for us – it seemed right. We knew that the right church home for our family was critical so we decided before moving that we would visit several churches. We visited Tabernacle — -and it felt right. When Kie Bowman, Tabernacle's Minister of Education, called us at our home in Kentucky after a visit to Tabernacle just to check on us and see if there was anything he could do – it felt right. When we would visit Tabernacle on the weekends as we searched for a home – it felt right. As we checked out many different houses and kept coming back to the house we own now – it felt right. Every step we took felt right. The people we came in contact with helped us in every way they could—extending and sharing God's love through their everyday actions – through the gifts and tools God had blessed them with in order to bless others.

Even though it all felt right – it was still very hard. The sadness felt as we pulled away from our home and friends in the little town of Eddyville, Kentucky penetrated the air. The question as to "why" was still unanswered.

Twenty years later we look back on that time and know God's hand was guiding us to this place. Gary and I truly feel God led us to Cartersville, Georgia not only for us to grow spiritually and be able to serve the Lord, but more importantly so our three girls could be brought up in the caring fellowship of a church like Tabernacle. Yes, they would have continued to grow in our previous church, but their experiences and opportunities would have been more limited. The pastors they have been privileged to "sit under" and be fed by, the patient youth leaders who have loved and guided them through the years, the varied music and performance opportunities they have benefited from, the Sunday School teachers who have loved them and taught them, the mission trips and Disciple Now week-ends that provided multiple opportunities to learn and share and grow have all contributed to their spiritual growth. The seeds were planted, watered, nourished, and continue to multiply and blossom as they each share what they have been taught with others. God is so good. *"For My thoughts are not your thoughts, neither are your ways My ways..."Isaiah 55:8*

We look forward as the boundaries of our family puzzle continue to expand with sons-in-law and precious grandbabies. God only knows the challenges and blessings in store for all of us as we continue to search for His will every step of the way.

"I can do all things through Him who strengthens me." **Philippians 4:13**

"...nothing is too difficult for Thee." **Jeremiah 32:17**

AMAZING GRACE
by
WANDA GRAY

*"Receive and experience the **amazing grace** of the Master, Jesus Christ, deep, deep within yourselves"* Philippians 4:23(MSG) (emphasis added)

I certainly have been putting this off for a very long time. Every time I think of getting started I always get side tracked and do something else. I believe it is hard for people to put down on paper their words and their feelings in general. Even when I try to let someone else know how MIGHTY AND POWERFUL the things are that God has done for me…it is just far too overwhelming. BUT, I am going to try because it important to my Christian life to actually hold myself accountable to GOD'S AMAZING GRACE! I do "color outside the lines"… so here I go…

My parents, Monroe and Faye Cagle, always took me to church at Tabernacle. For that I am truly thankful. I remember Mr. Joe Palmer holding me in pre-school Sunday School and showing me God's love. My pre-school department at Tabernacle was located on the first floor of what is now known as Bed Babies and 1 Year Olds in Pre-School Sunday School. (It is a good feeling that now GOD has given me the privilege to work with Tabernacle's Pre-School Sunday School because truly that was the beginning of my 'walk with JESUS.') At that time I truly believe it was much head knowledge...the heart change was to come. Thank you Pre-School Teachers for laying that foundation and Mom and Dad for taking me to church.

During revival on April 4, 1964 I walked the aisle and accepted JESUS as my personal Lord and Savior. I truly believe I was saved as a 9 year old at that time. I must admit now that JESUS started becoming REAL to me because I allowed HIM to become REAL to me as I continued to grow-up at Tabernacle. Mrs. Whitworth, Mrs. Cox, Mrs. Mary Lou and countless others (my children's department Sunday School teachers) continued to try to teach me about God's love and HIS AMAZING GRACE. I loved Vacation Bible School and GA's. Now, many of you might not know what GA's is but it stands for Girl's Auxiliary. We met each week and learned scriptures (which I use to this day) and did service projects to show others God's love. I remember those "sword drill" competitions. I loved to look up scripture. (Incidentally, my brother Cliff went to the State

Sword Drill competition in 1965.) Thank you Mom and Dad for taking me to church!

I was allowed to go on Youth Mission Trips and tried to introduce people to God's love but sometimes I was distracted by friends...especially boys. Being a teenager was a tough time for me but no one ever knew it. Wayne Stickler was our Youth Minister and I truly looked up to him and He taught me so much about how God wants us to serve HIM. I loved our youth get-togethers. I loved youth choir (I sang a lot of solos and played the piano but now I realize I was making a 'joyful noise')Thank you Mom and Dad for taking me to church!

As time went on I went off to college and definitely put God on a back burner. I did think I knew exactly what I wanted to do not realizing that God's plan for my life was transforming me. I went through many hard times crying out to God when the going was getting tough. I did, however, only cry out during the hard times. I had that Christian foundation and I am so thankful that Mom and Dad took me to church.

Just a few hard times <u>(there are so many I can't name them all)</u> to mention was the development of diabetes at the age of 22 when I first began teaching(1977). There were so many adjustments I had to make in my life. But I must say now HIS plan for my physical health was amazing because I am very grateful I do have a disease I can control and so far I am in better physical shape than I have ever been in. It is daily work for me to take care of my health and much of the time it is not easy but I started relying on God and that makes the hardships so much better. The death of my dad (1982- I was 27) and then the death of my mom(1987- I was 32) was devastating. I didn't have the relationship I wanted to have with my mom or dad but yet (That is a total book within itself!) I loved them. I do realize now the financial and time stresses that they had in their lives because of my brother and I. Even though I had a wonderful big brother, he was in the military traveling constantly so I spent a number of Christmases and birthdays alone. Now don't feel too sad for me. During those alone times GOD really spoke to me and I started to allow HIM to finally work in my life. Thank you Mom and Dad for taking me to church!

God allowed me to meet my husband Steve in Tabernacle's Singles Department in 1990 and we married in 1991. AND yes, we have struggled like every other married couple. Keeping God first is, above all, the most important thing in any relationship. I have realized that I need to rely on GOD'S AMAZING GRACE and HIS faithfulness. (I keep using that don't I?) Thank you Mom and Dad for taking me to church? (HAHA)

God spoke to me during a church musical "GOD WITH US." I believe I truly surrendered that night to what God wanted me to do. I always tried to help HIM with my life and there was really no peace, so I finally surrendered and my life has never been the same. I have a peace that surpasses all understanding along with such a wonderful church family that holds me accountable to what God has **still** planned for my life. I am excited every morning to see what God has for me.

It ALL began when my parents took me (and made me) go to church; to Tabernacle's Pre-School, Children's, Youth, Young Adult, and Adult Sunday School, and when I allowed God to enter my life. My story of faith does not end here because there is so much more…so ask me sometime if you want to hear more of God's Amazing Grace in my life!

THANK YOU TABERNACLE, BUT ABOVE
ALL........THANK YOU JESUS!

ABOVE AND BEYOND
by
JOHN GRESH

❦

"God can do anything, you know—far more than you could ever imagine or guess or request in your wildest dreams! He does it not by pushing us around but by working within us, his Spirit deeply and gently within us."
Ephesians 3:20 (MSG)

During the summer of 1999, money was next to non-existent in my family. There was no savings or checking or assets. My business had gone bust as a roofing contractor, and the debts were more than we could pay back. To make matters worse, my ankle was severely sprained, making roofing an impossibility for my physically.

Then…the **miracles** started…You see, several months earlier, I had given my life to Jesus Christ. I was baptized on Easter Sunday, 1999.

After injuring my ankle, I was hired by Thrall Car in Cartersville to work as a laborer in the fabrication shop. This was extremely heavy and dangerous work for a young man, let alone a guy my age of 50 years. The day of my hiring physical, my ankle swelling was gone and I was able to walk without any problem! **THEN,** after three months on the job, a $500 bonus was given to the employees in my department.

My daughter, Monica, had just graduated from Cass High School. She was praying to attend Liberty University, but the cost was prohibitive even with an available scholarship. Steve McCombs, the youth minister at Tabernacle, was able to arrange a campus interview for Monica with Truett McConnell College in Cleveland, GA. The time frame was now July/early August. School would be in session in two weeks.

As we toured the TMC campus, I was thinking there was no way for us to afford the tuition, books, room and board at this private college. Then another miracle happened.

We "happened" to go through the gymnasium and met the women's basketball coach. She was rather forlorn because a scholarship to play basketball was rejected at the last minute. This would leave her squad one short for the coming season. When the coach discovered that Monica was a four-year letterman in basketball, she offered the scholarship to Monica on the spot! Although Monica played varsity basketball four years at Cass High, we never thought she would go beyond that…God had other plans!

With less than two weeks before the start of school, Monica now had a "full ride" – tuition, books, room and board at Truett McConnell!

Two weeks later, Monica called home. A foul-up in the paperwork for her scholarship occurred and she needed to pay $450 immediately or be ineligible to attend class.

Remember my $500 bonus from earlier?? Well, guess what...I had tithed $50 to God and had **exactly** $450 which we had not spent. I was able to send it to Monica. Three weeks later, she called home again very excited. All her scholarship money had finally been processed and it was more than what the expenses were...so...$450 back to Monica!

My reaction, "Praise the Lord! He will provide ALL our needs!" I told Monica that we had now recouped the original $450. She said, "No, not really". See, she had felt compelled to wait on the Lord and had never even submitted the $450 check I had sent. The bottom line – God blessed us double with $900 on a $450 investment in a Christian Education.

P.S. Monica met a Chinese professor at TMC and became convicted to do two short-term missions to China and one to Taiwan. God truly blessed our family and provided for us above what we ever imagined!

CLAIRE'S MIRACLE
by
SUSAN HATFIELD

"Is any one of you sick? He should call the elders of the church to pray over him and anoint him with oil in the name of the Lord. And the prayer offered in faith will make the sick person well; the Lord will raise him up. If he has sinned, he will be forgiven. Therefore confess your sins to each other and pray for each other so that you may be healed. The prayer of a righteous man is powerful and effective."
James 5:14-16

When I read about the opportunity to share a testimony for this book, I thought, "Where should I begin?" God has blessed my family and me in so many ways. There are really so many testimonies to share!! I did, however, know that this was a wonderful opportunity to share one particular miracle that God performed in our family.

Hoyt and I have been tremendously blessed with 3 great children. Harrison, now 16, Holden who is 13 and Claire who is 10. In 1997, when Claire was 12 months old, she was diagnosed with neurofibromatosis. This is a genetic disorder which causes, among other things, tumors to grow on the nerves of the body. The doctors sent us to specialists in Atlanta. MRIs were scheduled to detect any brain tumors. We were immediately surrounded by friends and family who began praying for Claire and her health.

The first MRI was scheduled for February. We drew on the knowledge that God was in control as we anticipated the first test. The results of the test detected a tumor on her left optic nerve. We were told that there was no cure for NF. Subsequent MRIs every six months would be conducted to monitor the growth of this tumor and to detect others that might appear.

After much research, I learned that these tumors may lie dormant or begin to grow – never to go away. Depending on the location, surgery, radiation or chemotherapy could be required.

The next MRI was scheduled for May. One morning as I was reading my Bible and praying, God led me to **James 5:14-16** which reads, *"Is any one of you sick? He should call the elders of the church to pray over him and anoint him with oil in the name of the Lord. And the prayer offered in faith will make the sick person well; the Lord will raise him up. If he has sinned, he will be forgiven. 16Therefore confess your sins to each other and pray for each other so that* *you may be healed. The prayer of a righteous man is powerful and effective."* It was no coincidence that someone shared that same verse with Hoyt on that **same day!** We knew that God was leading us to have the deacons of our church pray for our daughter.

Hoyt called to have it arranged. It was a very special night – one that I will always remember. That evening, one by one, our home was filled with godly men who lifted Claire up in prayer. What a sense of peace and God's love we experienced!

Six months later, another MRI was conducted. The tumor had not grown. How thankful we were as we continued to pray. Six months later, the next MRI took place. The results of this test detected no tumors. **The tumor was gone!**

The specialists in Atlanta, as well as our doctors here, weren't sure what to say. We, however, knew exactly what to say. Praise God!! Although Claire was receiving no medicine or treatment, she was receiving prayer, which is really the most powerful medicine of all!!

We will be eternally thankful to God for performing this miracle, but let's not forget that He performs miracles in all our lives daily, simply by giving us life and blessing us with family and friends and so many other things that we forget to be thankful for. I am certain He performs miracles in our lives that we may never be aware of.

Claire continues with her yearly MRIs. While this disorder has presented some challenges to her, we know that God is in full control and will use this situation for good!

FAITH OVER FEAR
by
PASTOR DON HATTAWAY

"For God hath not given us the spirit of fear; but of power, and of love, and of a sound mind"
II Timothy 1:7 (KJV)

Born to Ethridge and June Hattaway in Douglas, Georgia on April 27, 1964, I was the only son of four children. My parents named me Ethridge Donald Hattaway after my daddy. We lived in a modest country home where my mama's chief concern was to take care of her husband and children. My daddy worked at Daniel's Feed and Seed and tended the small farm that we called home. Ours was a loving Christian home where we had many happy times together.

Our entire week revolved around a little country church called Harmony Grove Baptist. We faithfully attended Sunday mornings, evenings, and Wednesday night prayer meetings. My mama was the church pianist and my daddy was the song leader.

My parent's faith had a great impression on me. Through their Christian influence and the ministries of our church, I realized that I needed to have my own personal relationship with God. At age seven, I talked with my parents about becoming a Christian. After accepting Christ, I was baptized and began a journey of faith that has led me to where I am today.

Early in my life, God gave me a desire to be a preacher. I did not understand everything involved in that calling, but I knew that God had His hand on my life. Throughout my childhood and teenage years, God continued to guide me into vocational ministry. As I matured, I was rather shy about sharing my calling for fear that I might be unable to fulfill God's intention for me. During this time, God continued to confirm His plan for my life through a growing desire to be used by Him, a recognition of spiritual gifts needed to be a pastor, the encouragement of mature believers around me, godly counsel from my pastor, and opportunities to minister that only God could have provided.

Even with all these confirmations, I was still afraid of failure. I started college with the intent to wait for more confirmation from God before I fully started down the path to becoming a pastor. I became more involved in the church where I was attending, including joining the choir. God opened many new doors through my service in the church. One day a minister of music suggested that I attend Brewton-Parker College to major in music. Not fully understanding what I was getting into, I applied and was accepted. Shortly after, God provided many opportunities for me to minister through song and sermon.

Slowly, God directed me away from a music ministry and into the role of a pastor. At this point, I had matured enough to realize that when God calls He also provides the resources to accomplish the work. I had discovered that my ability to succeed in the ministry was not determined by my strength, but in His strength.

After finishing college, attending seminary, and ministering in three churches for the last 25 years, I am a living testimony of God's ability to use a simple, shy boy to serve the King of kings and the Lord of lords.

AMAZING GRACE
by
SONNY HATTAWAY

"Blessed is the man who perseveres under trial, because when he has stood the test, he will receive the crown of life that God has promised to those who love him."
James 1:12

At the young age of six I accepted Christ as my Savior. The journey of my Christian faith has been just that—a journey. Though there are many experiences I could share, there is one significant time in my life that was most pivotal. I can recall a point in my life where I experienced God's grace in an extraordinary way. This occurred during my college years before I met my Don. I attended a Georgia Baptist College, which was supposed to help me continue in my growth and knowledge of the Scriptures.

Unfortunately, liberalism had permeated through this college. I sat under professors who told me they believed that everyone was going to Heaven, that hell was not an actual place, and that Satan was not an actual person—only that a strong force of evil existed. This is one of many false doctrines that I was taught through my early years of college. I had been raised in a strong Christian home and I knew these things were ludicrous, but because I allowed myself to be swayed by friends' beliefs and the beliefs of some professors that I respected, I began to question the God that I had lived for all my life.

Through a period of time I struggled greatly with the faith I held—even to the point of wondering if the God I had served was really **real**. I can remember an actual week of intense struggle when I knew that I had to choose between following God or going the world's way. Praise be to God—He made Himself known to me and I knew that I could not leave the God I loved. Looking back, I can now see the strong attack of Satan on my life. I know now that Satan was doing all he could to keep me from what God had in store for my life.

If I had chosen to walk away from my faith, I would never have married Don, never would have become a pastor's wife, and never devoted myself to full-time ministry. Because of God's **grace,** God's **faithfulness,** and God's **enduring love** for me, I returned to Him with an even deeper love and gratitude for all that He's done—for saving me, for waiting on me while I wandered, for giving me an abundant life worth living. There have been countless times through my spiritual journey that God's grace has covered me, and I can truly say that even to this day...His grace still amazes me.

AN AWESOME GOD
by
SUE HEDDEN

"How awesome is the Lord Most High, the great King over all the earth!"
Psalm 47:2

My husband, Donald, was born and raised on a farm in Blairsville, Georgia. At the age of 12, he accepted Jesus as his Lord and Savior during a revival at Pleasant Grove Baptist Church in Blairsville. Donald was 17 years old when he and his family left Blairsville and moved to Cartersville. A short time later they moved to Murphy, North Carolina where Donald graduated. Soon after graduation, Donald moved to Atlanta to get a job, and began working for the Gulf Oil Corporation at the station across from the Varsity, training to be a salesman.

December 12, 1961 was a very cold and rainy winter night. He had been to the Varsity to eat and was almost across the street when a 1958 Impala Chevrolet, driven by a drunk driver, ran a stop sign and hit him. He was thrown to the crosswalk at North Avenue and Spring Street. His right leg was broken three times below the knee and his left leg two times below the knee.

An Army officer and his wife were at the station and saw the accident. He went to Donald and put his raincoat over him. We will forever be grateful to him. The ambulance came and took Donald to Grady Hospital and later he was transferred to Dekalb General Hospital, which was a new hospital. Dr. Baker Huff, a Christian, was his doctor.

At the time, Donald's family lived in North Carolina, but immediately came to Atlanta. When they arrived at the hospital, they were told his right leg would have to be amputated, but Donald told them no way. Miracles began happening. Thanks be to God! He spent Christmas and New Year's in the hospital. Thirty days later he went back home to North Carolina. Dr. Baker Huff told Donald, a higher power saved his leg. To God be the glory!!

At the time of the accident, Donald and I were engaged to be married in June 1962, but our wedding was postponed to November 1962.

I visited Donald often while he was in the hospital and my sister, Bettie, and I spent the weekend with Donald and his family in North Carolina.

Nine months later Donald went back to work, but couldn't stand working on the "rock" as it was called. Gulf Oil Corporation gave him a job in the office at the corner of 17th and West Peachtree Street and he stayed there until he retired in 1985. (He was the supervisor over the computer room and a pricing analysis. We do not even have a computer.)

He went into business for himself – Don's Lawn Service. After 21 years, we sold our business in March 2007 and retired again. God is an awesome God! Keep your faith and talk to God often.

THE CHRISTMAS TREE
by
NANCY HIGGINBOTHAM

"Delight yourself in the LORD and he will give you the desires of your heart."
Psalm 37:4

Christmas has always been my favorite time of the year, both as a child and as an adult. The sights and smells of Christmas create a sense of wonder and excitement that can't be matched any other time of year. This is the time we celebrate the birth of our Savior. Even though there are those who try to take Christ out of Christmas, there is always someone keeping Him in the center of it all. So here is my Christmas tree story.

It was December 1991 and Gary had just changed jobs. He was a car salesman and a new Christian. As a car salesman he was paid by commission only. At this time, I was making $50 a week by babysitting two children on weekdays. November was not a good month for Gary. He brought home a check for about $300. This wasn't much money for a family of five renting an apartment in Memphis, Tennessee. Aubrey was seven, Ashley was five, and Austin was two.

God had been teaching us many lessons that past year and we knew He was faithful and had promised to take care of us. Gary decided we wouldn't tell anyone about our financial situation except God. So we prayed and trusted God to see us through. I'm still amazed at how God worked in our life and built our faith. We received checks in the mail from family who told us God had laid us on their heart and just sent the money. We praised God for His faithfulness! That first weekend Gary's parents came to visit and brought a huge cooler of vegetables, meat, and fruit they had in their freezer. We praised God for His faithfulness!

Around the first of December, I asked Gary if we were going to have a Christmas tree that year. I almost felt guilty asking because I knew our money situation, but every day I also looked into the faces of three excited children who wondered when we would put up our tree. We always got a real tree and didn't have an artificial tree stored somewhere. Needless to say, Gary said we couldn't afford a tree. So I went to God and poured out my heart to Him. Praying for food, shelter, and clothing to a God Who loved me and promised to take care of me was easy. I trusted God to provide those things. But a Christmas tree was a luxury. Not that I didn't trust God to provide us with a Christmas tree, but it was not a need in our lives. I let Him know this and prayed for it anyway. I wanted this for my children most of all.

One Saturday morning a couple of weeks later, I was still talking to God about the Christmas tree and I remember praying that if He provided a tree then it was fine and also if He didn't it was fine. After my quiet time that morning, I had decided to tell the kids, when they asked again, that we weren't going to have a tree that year.

Gary went to work as usual that morning and the kids got up one by one and had breakfast. Then the question came. When are we going to get our Christmas tree? I gathered them all around to talk to them and just as I opened my mouth to speak, there was a knock at the door. I went to answer it and it was our neighbor. He said he felt funny asking me this, but did I have a Christmas tree? I told him I didn't. Well, while he was out cutting their Christmas tree, God laid us on his heart and he cut us one too! This neighbor let God be in the center of his life. He didn't know I was praying for a Christmas tree at the time, but he was still obedient to God's voice.

Praise God for His faithfulness! I learned God is more than a God that provides for our needs. He cares about each of us on a personal basis. Every time I see a Christmas tree I'm reminded of this.

DESIRES OF MY HEART
by
JENNIE HORTON

"Delight yourself also in the Lord and He shall give you the desires of your heart."
Psalm 37:4

I've often wondered, if this Scripture meant that as we delight in the Lord, He will place certain **desires** in our heart or that because we delight in Him, He will give us the **desires** of our heart?

Growing up, a great **desire** in my heart was to get married, have a family, and be able to stay home with my children. Late in my teen years, that hope and dream was dashed. I was diagnosed with acute endometriosis, a condition that can cause infertility. By my early twenties, and several surgeries later, I was told that I may never be able to have children.

I was sad, but there was no way I could have fully understood that diagnosis at the time. I was young, having fun, and filling my life and time with other things, not yet desiring to have a child.

Eric and I were married January 19, 1990. We were not married long before the **desire** to have children flooded my heart. We tried many different procedures with doctors that specialized in infertility, but to no avail. And for the first time, I began to understand the depth of what the doctors had told me years earlier.

The heartbreak of a shattered dream was at times too much to bear, all the while wondering where God was in the midst of this storm. We had come to the conclusion that we would never have children and that we should just move on with our lives. My doctor ordered an endometrial biopsy to further diagnose a recurring condition. Prior to having this procedure a pregnancy test is given because it is likely to cause a miscarriage when performed. There was not even the slightest thought that it would be positive and sure enough it was not.

The very day that I was having this procedure done, unbeknown to us, my grandmother was listening to IBN, Immanuel Broadcast Network (our local Christian radio station). A man was sharing his family's personal story about infertility. As the program came to an end, they had a special time of prayer for those who were struggling with this heartbreak and pain. My grandmother stopped what she was doing and stood in the gap for us praying and pleading with God on our behalf.

A few days later when my cycle was not what it should have been, I decided to take the last pregnancy test that we had purchased. And to my thrill it was positive. I went straight to the doctor's office for the official confirmation. I was pregnant, against medical expectations and all odds!

We had an upcoming family get together and knew that it would be the perfect night to tell everyone. As we shared our exciting news, my grandmother started to weep for she remembered the prayer that was offered up on our behalf. Upon sharing the details, we figured out she was praying on the exact day and same time that I was having my biopsy.

It was a blissful pregnancy and on February 10, 1993 our MIRACLE #1, Hunter Cole Horton, was born. Thank you, Jesus!

We enjoyed the thrill of parenthood, but as Hunter got older our desire to fill our home with another child grew. Back to the doctors! There we were again, disappointment after disappointment. In 1996 I had to have a hysterectomy. We reconciled ourselves to the fact that our family would be what it was, a family of three. Heartbroken, disappointed, and somewhat angry, I had to work through emotions that I was not ready to work through.

During a follow up visit with my doctor, he asked me if we had considered adoption. I shared my fears that came mostly from two highly publicized cases in which the children were being taken from the adoptive families. He, being an adoptive parent himself, explained to me that those adoptions were faulty from the beginning. Adoptions done in the right legal order would be fine. This kindled a spark of hope that maybe we could enlarge our family. We privately pondered the thought, not knowing where to even begin.

Again, unbeknown to us, the Lord had laid our names on the heart of the director of the Pregnancy Care Center (now Bartow County Women's Resource Center). We were acquaintances, but she had no idea what we had been through or that we were even thinking about adoption. (I love it when God is working behind the scenes!) At a non-coincidental meeting, the director shared her heart with me. She felt very strongly that we would adopt a baby through the Center. WOW! Could this really be the avenue that God was allowing us to go down?

Soon after the idea had taken birth in our hearts, we received a call from the director. She had a young couple that needed to put their baby up for adoption and they wanted to meet us. With great anticipation and excitement we met them, but within minutes we knew that this was not going to work out. The father was an atheist and he asked in depth questions about how this child would be raised spiritually. We wanted this so badly and as tempting as it was to just be quiet so that he would like us, we knew that we could not deny Christ. They left and they denied us. Heartbroken again, we wondered why.

Several months went by before we got another call. This young girl came from a mixed up family and had been abandoned by the birth father. She loved us and wanted us for her child. But there was something that just wasn't right and we could not get a peace about it. So as difficult as it was, we had to say no to her. Why, God, why?

Infertility is such an emotional roller coaster. I thought I had gotten off this ride when I had my hysterectomy. Now, the adoption process had me back on it. Over the next few months, we received more calls, none of which worked out. Why, God, why?

In March of 1998, I went to a ladies' retreat. Emotionally, I was in a valley that I never thought I would come out of. I was there only to get away from everything, not even expecting or looking for anything spiritually. There was a door prize table that I had noticed. I walked over to it and told the man standing there that if he drew names, I wanted him to draw mine because I never won anything and I wanted a prize. He asked me if I minded him praying for me about the prize. A little shocked and taken aback, I giggled and said, "Sure, you can pray for me." He said the sweetest prayer about my getting a prize.

When he finished praying, the hair on his arms was standing straight up. He wanted to know how many children I had. I told him only one. He said, "Ma'am, you have another one on the way. When you get that baby and you kiss its face you will know that is your prize." My friends and I just started crying. They all knew what I was going through, but this man did not know me, nor did he know anything about my past. We, through prayer and supplication, had an experience with God. One of my friends spoke up and asked, "When?" He said, "It won't be long."

I went home revived, refreshed, hopeful, and full of faith that this would come to pass. In July 1998, I met a young girl who needed to put her baby up for adoption. She herself had been the product of a rape. She had never known of a father's love and because of this she desperately wanted her child to be raised in a loving Christian home with a father. She had hopes and dreams for her child that she knew she could not meet. So she selflessly chose us to be the family that would have the privilege of raising her baby. She included me in all of the remainder of the doctor visits and allowed me to be at the hospital when Chandler Wade Horton, MIRACLE, #2 was born. Might I add, exactly nine months later than when the "door prize man" prayed for me.

I didn't like what I went through at the time that I was going through it, but I wouldn't change it for the world. God knows best. He's got a plan and His timing is perfect. He parted my Red Sea. He healed my broken heart. He opened my blind eyes to His will and way. He has given me the **desires** of my heart and I will forever be grateful.

THE MIRACLE OF THE HOT WATER BOTTLE
Submitted by
KATHY HOWREN

"Before they call, I will answer."
Isaiah 65:25

This story was given to me by a very special daughter of a friend of mine at a time when I needed it most. It is the story of a doctor who was serving God in South Africa as told from his perspective. I hope it will be a blessing to you...

One night I had worked hard to help a mother in the labor ward, but in spite of all we could do, she died leaving us with a premature baby and a crying 2 year old daughter. Although we lived on the equator, nights were chilly with tremendous drafts. We had no electricity to run an incubator...even if we had one...so keeping the baby alive would be a difficult task.

A student mid-wife wrapped the baby as best she could, while another went to fill a hot water bottle. To our dismay, the hot water bottle burst as it was being filled. It was our only hot water bottle!

We placed the baby close to the fire and a midwife lay between the baby and the door to keep it from drafts. The orphanage children had heard about the birth of this new baby and the heartbroken 2 year old girl. They gathered around me for words of encouragement and a time of prayer. I explained the situation to them mentioning the hot water bottle and that without it the baby could easily die. I also told them about the sister crying because she had lost her mother.

One little girl named Ruth stepped forward and prayed aloud very bluntly, as African children often do, "Please God, send us a hot water bottle TODAY. It will be no good tomorrow, God, as the baby will be dead. So...please send it this afternoon!"

While I gasped at the prayer of this child's heart, she continued with clarity, "and while You are about it, would You please send a dolly for the little girl so she will know You really love her?"

As often with children's prayers, I was put on the spot. Could I honestly say, "amen"? I guess I just did not believe God could do this. Oh yes, I know that He can do everything. The Bible says so, but there are limits aren't there? The only way God could answer this prayer would be for a package to arrive. I had been in Africa for four years and I never received a parcel from home. And besides, if someone DID send a package, who would include a hot water bottle? I lived on the equator!

Halfway through the afternoon a message was sent to me that a car was in front of my door. By the time I reached home, the car was gone, but there on the porch lay a 22 pound package. I felt tears pricking my eyes. I could not open this package alone, so I called for the orphanage children. This was such a special moment.

As 40 pairs of eyes focused intently on the box, we opened it to reveal many brightly colored jerseys. I passed them out and their eyes sparkled. Next came much needed medical and food supplies.

Then, as I put my hand in again, I felt the…could it really be? I grasped it, pulled it out and began to weep uncontrollably. It was a brand new rubber hot water bottle!!

I had not asked God to send it; I had not really believed that He could. But Ruth, a small orphan girl in Africa had sincerely prayed asking God to send provisions for this newborn baby and God had answered in perfect timing! I knew I had experienced a miracle and the power of prayer. My heart was overflowing with thanksgiving and gratitude to an awesome God!

However, in the majesty of that moment, Ruth pushed her way forward toward the box. She began digging through it fiercely saying, "If God has sent that hot water bottle, He must have sent that dolly too! THAT was my prayer." Rummaging down to the bottom of the box, she pulled out the small beautifully dressed doll. She **never doubted.**

Looking up at me she asked, "Can I go with you to give this dolly to that little girl so she will know that Jesus loves her?"

That parcel had been on its way for five whole months, packed by a Sunday School class whose leader had heard and obeyed God's prompting to send a hot water bottle to the equator! One of those girls had lovingly placed a doll in the box, five months earlier, in answer to the believing prayer of a ten year old girl named Ruth who asked God to "bring it this afternoon."

Dear one, what is your hot water bottle?

THE POWER OF PRAYER
by
Kathy Howren

"Is any one of you sick? He should call the elders of the church to pray over him and anoint him with oil in the name of the Lord. And the prayer offered in faith will make the sick person well."
James 5:14

On May 6, 2002 I was diagnosed with bilateral simultaneous lung cancer. (Meaning an identical mass in each lung.) It is rare and generally effects non-smoking women. The doctors also found a questionable lymph node that strongly appeared to be cancerous. I was in a state of shock. All of this had been discovered through a routine doctor's visit and chest x-rays that I had personally requested due to a chronic cough.

My family, Michael, Paige, Ansley and Mike, had the responsibility of making most of the decisions during that time. I was hardly able to function, but I knew that God was my refuge and strength and He was ever present in our hour of need.

Michael and I firmly believe the Word of God and the power of prayer. **James 5:13-15** clearly tells us what we are to do: *"Is any one of you in trouble? He should pray. Is anyone happy? Let him sing songs of praise. Is any one of you sick? He should call the elders of the church to pray over him and anoint him with oil in the name of the Lord. And the prayer offered in faith will make the sick person well; the Lord will raise him up. If he has sinned, he will be forgiven. Therefore confess your sins to each other and pray for each other so that you may be healed. The prayer of a righteous man is powerful and effective."*

On May 11, we met in the sanctuary at Tabernacle with our children, the deacon body and their wives. I was prayed for and anointed with oil in obedience to the scriptures. It was the most humbling experience of my life. As we left that day, the heavy burden was lifted from our shoulders and placed into the hands of God. **Ps. 68:19-20** says

"Blessed be the Lord who daily bears our burden. The Lord who is our salvation!"

May 13th began a series of extensive tests to confirm whether or not the cancer had spread to other parts of my body. Many days were full of scans at Emory or Crawford Long Hospital. If you have ever experienced these lengthy scans, you know that you are flat on your back. **Psalm 91** became very special to me and I relied on that passage.

Five days before surgery on June 5th, we went to Crawford Long for the last series of tests which were a MRI and bone scan. Around 3:00, my family and I went in to Dr. Miller's office to hear news we did not expect. The bone scan revealed that the cancer had spread to my spinal column. Devastated, we were sent back to Radiology for further examinations and review by a team of orthopedic specialists. After many hours of waiting, Dr. Miller's assistant came through the waiting room door all smiles, giving us the "2 thumbs up"! He said, "Little lady, you have arthritis." Arthritis never sounded so good! I would still be scheduled for surgery to address the identical masses in my lungs.

June 10th I underwent surgery at Crawford Long Hospital. My family and so many precious friends were there. Most importantly, GOD was there! I felt His presence in such a mighty way.

The first part of the surgery was to address the questionable lymph node. Hallelujah! It proved to be infected, not cancerous. This allowed surgery to be done to remove the lower lobe of my right lung housing a malignant tumor. Our prayers had been answered. We felt so blessed.

Before going to surgery, I had told Dr. Miller that we believed in the power of prayer and that so many people were praying for me and for him as well. I will never forget his response. He said, "My hands are only a tool for God to use, and I believe in prayer too."

After a very successful surgery, I was told that I would have the 2nd surgery on my left lung in 6-

8 weeks. I continued with the scans and x-rays. On November 11, 2002, I went to Dr. Miller to review my tests and schedule the 2nd surgery. Dr. Miller showed us the early scans which <u>clearly and unmistakably</u> showed two mirror-image tumors on the right and left lungs. THEN, he put up the new scans for Michael and I to see. The right lung was visibly shortened by the previous surgery and the left lung was CLEAR, HEALTHY and as Dr. Miller said, "**unexplainably tumor free**"!

We both knew the answer to this mysterious healing. Through prayer, God had used the hands of this willing servant for healing in my right lung. But God was not finished! He had, without the use of human hands, miraculously healed my left lung!

This was a gift from God's heart in answer to so many prayers. My family and I were deeply humbled by the love of our wonderful church family and our dear friends. We thank our wonderful Lord and we thank you for believing with us and for praying without ceasing.

If you read the story I submitted just before this one entitled, *The Miracle of the Hot Water Bottle*, you realize, I received my "water bottle" thanks to the prayers of so many of you. You were my "Ruth".

God is an awesome God! I share this testimony only to give Him praise, honor and glory. In closing, my family and I would like to share this prayer based on **Psalm 31:20-22.**

Our soul waits for the Lord,
He is our help and our shield.
For our hearts rejoice in Him
Because we trust in His holy name.
Let Thy loving kindness, O Lord, be upon us
According as we have hoped in Thee

May God bless each of you and continue to use you to bless others.

THREE BEAN SALAD
by
CAREN KELLEY

*"**Give freely** and spontaneously. Don't have a stingy heart. The way you handle matters like this triggers God, your God's, blessing in everything you do, all your work and ventures. There are always going to be poor and needy people among you. So I command you: Always be generous, open purse and hands, **give to your neighbors** in trouble, your poor and hurting neighbors"*
Deuteronomy 15:10 (MSG) (emphasis added)

It was the first Thanksgiving that my sons (ages 2, 10 and 14) and I were going to spend alone. It was a pretty bleak time. I worked two jobs and then two nights a week the boys and I prepared the church for Wednesday and Sunday services. Either Steve or Chris would watch Scotty, who was just two, in the nursery at church while the other son would help me clean.

The first of November we started noticing a basket in the foyer of the church with a sign that said, "Please donate groceries to a needy family." As it got closer to Thanksgiving, my sons asked, "Mama, what are we going to give?" Our pantry was empty except for a can of "Three Bean Salad". We didn't know where it came from and really didn't know what to do with it.

We knew we had to give sacrificially. The Monday before Thanksgiving, my oldest two emptied their wallet and piggy banks as we headed for the grocery store. They each bought things with their own money for the needy family. We took our donation to the church on Tuesday night where the boys happily put in their food, along with the can of "Three Bean Salad".

Wednesday night we heard a noise in our driveway and looked out to see the church van and several friends carrying boxes to our front door. We had no idea what was about to happen, but as we opened the front door, they all yelled, "Happy Thanksgiving!" My goodness...**we were the needy family** and didn't even know it!

Sitting on top of one of the many boxes overflowing with delicious canned goods was a can of... you guessed it..."Three Bean Salad". We got it back and we still did not know what to do with it!

That first year was so hard as I was learning to be the head of the household and the bread winner. We faced so many challenges. What we lacked financially was made up by God's grace and everlasting love and the love and generosity of our church family. Money can't buy what we had that year. Now that the boys are all grown, we all still remember that year…our worst-best-year ever! Every time we hear "Three Bean Salad", we smile.

BLESSED ASSURANCE
by
DARLA LARUE

"And this is the secret: Christ lives in you. This gives you assurance of sharing his glory."
Colossians 1:27 (NLT)

If we are saved by grace through Jesus Christ we have a testimony. Each one is different and the road we travel to get to the point of repentance is different, but the end result for each is that of becoming a born again Christian.

As my story unfolds, you will realize my testimony deals with my will vs. God's will....and my mind vs. God's heart. I believe that is a terrible struggle for each of us. We are to have no will of our own but are to seek God's will in all we do. **I John 5:14** says, *"And this is the confidence that we have in Him, that if we ask anything according to His will, He will hear us."* You notice that it doesn't say, "according to my will." You see.....this battle was a mighty one for me.

I was raised by Christian parents and church was a major part of our lives. At the age of 14, during a revival service, I told God he needed to save me. I proceeded to tell Him how, where, and under what conditions. I prayed and felt better. This was good, I thought. At the age of 19 I married a young man who was also 19. He was raised in church as well. As a young couple our church attendance was very hit and miss. After seven years we were expecting our first child. We knew we needed to raise our child in church, so we began to attend regularly at a Baptist church. Some friends had invited us and we joined soon after. In three years, our second child was born. A few months later my husband was transferred to the Woodstock area, so we left everything we knew in Chattanooga and moved to a new home and a whole new life. One year later, our third child was born. By this time we were totally out of church.

Over the years, every once in a while, there would be a tug at my heart. It was a tug I could not understand. There was an emptiness I could not put my finger on. I blamed it on having three children, living in a new place, my husband, his job, and even not having a church home.

After a few years, we met a couple and became friends. They invited us to Tabernacle and we went. After a few weeks we joined. Finally, we were doing the right thing. We were very regular in our attendance in both Sunday School and church. Regardless...that same uneasy nagging feeling continued. I started to question my salvation at times. Oh...I knew what I needed. I needed more involvement, so I got involved. I love to decorate, so decorated everything for almost every church function that came along. I started singing in the choir. I began working with the youth. This was good....I was doing God's work!

Through God's grace and love, I started hearing things that cut through to my heart. In choir practice, Brother Don Startup would take time out to minister to us from the scriptures and through testimonies. Our pastor at that time would preach messages on church members needing to get saved. I thought this was crazy. Nevertheless, revivals would come along and we would hear the same thing. Gradually, the wall around my heart began to crumble. I would wake up during the night in a cold sweat, gripped with uncontrolled fear. "What if I'm not saved?" I thought. Well that was ridiculous! I could remember the time when I was 14 and had said a prayer. I thought, "Well, if I'm not saved, God will just have to save me at home. There was no way I will ever go forward during an invitation at church. I'm not going to be baptized again either. Everyone thinks I'm already a Christian so they will never know the difference."

I'd like to say right here that this statement alone proved how foolish I was.

There is a difference......Thank God! You see, I did not want to look like a fool. I was worried about what everybody would think. Satan knows our weaknesses and fears and how to manipulate and deceive each of us. In the midst of all of this, something inside of me would say, "You're ok...everything is fine...just forget it," but I could not. I was miserable.

In April of 1996 we had a revival at Tabernacle. On Sunday morning the sermon was entitled, "Are You Sure of Your Salvation?" The preacher said, "If you are even 1% unsure, something isn't right." Well, panic struck me. God continued to pull at my heart. In the Sunday night service it was basically the same message. On Monday night, I didn't return. I was filled with a combination of anger and fear. After I put the kids to bed that night I tried to pray but I couldn't. I tried to read my Bible but could not. I cannot even begin to describe the ache in my heart and the sadness that I felt.

I remembered at different times in choir practice, Brother Don would say, "You cannot ask to be saved until you know you are lost!" My husband had to work late that night. When he arrived home, he took one look at me knew something was terribly wrong. I explained to him, the best I could, what was going on with me. He was shocked. I had managed to hide the inner turmoil well. Funny thing is...he was having similar feelings which is a whole different wonderful story. (Be sure to read Mike's story!)

The next day we went together to see Brother Don. I knew from his own testimony that he had been there and that maybe he would have some answers for us. He asked us, "Are you willing to do whatever God wants you to do?" Oh wow! This was scary. Me, do whatever God wanted? At this point, my answer was, "yes." I was miserable and was ready for whatever it took. Don then spoke of God's peace. This broke my heart for I knew there was no peace in my life.

The next day was Wednesday and I was determined to get answers. I got in my car and drove around town. There was no radio on. It was just me begging for God's help. I could not continue in the shape I was in because I was sick and desperate. I then headed down I-75 and realized I was ready for any answer God had for me. I was gripping the steering wheel, crying, and just pleading to God. I know other people on the freeway must have thought I was a crazy woman. Suddenly, a voice came to me just as plain as day. "Be still, be quiet, and calm. God will let you know. He is kind, gentle, and He is love." I actually answered back, "Okay." A calmness washed over me and I was more relaxed than I had been in days. I knew God would help me.

I drove about three more miles down the road. Suddenly, like getting hit with a brick, and as if someone were in the car with me, I heard someone say, "Remember when you were 14 and you called out to be saved? You never had the faith that I could do what I said I would. Then you remembered the scriptures. For whosoever shall call upon the name of the Lord shall be saved. You never asked! You never finished what you started."

As the Holy Spirit spoke to me, it all came flooding back as if it were yesterday. Not just the words that came from my mouth, but also my attitude. I was stubborn. Not only was church a major part of our lives, but I was a preacher's kid. It always seemed like more was expected of me than others. That was not fair. As far as my salvation was concerned, I would do it my way, when I was ready. No one would make me do any different. Yes, I was under conviction but God was going to have to save me at home with no one around. I was shy also. There was no way I would go down to an altar and kneel down to pray to God in front of everybody.

As I drove down the road I realized that I had plenty of "attitude" and no "willingness" to surrender to God. I was not humble in the least. That day when I was 14, I had asked God to save me but I gave up on Him. I then remembered **Romans 10:13**, *"Whosoever shall call upon the name of the Lord shall be saved."* Oh, I was excited, but I mistook emotion and knowledge for salvation. Oh yes, I had prayed and demanded, but it is not the words that come from our mouths that count, but the condition of our hearts. God looks past our mouths and directly into our hearts! You see, I never surrendered to Him on that day. It was so simple, yet left so undone. All of those years were laid out before me. Now the missing piece was revealed. Suddenly, I knew I was lost!

A fear shook me. I was without Christ! I could not get back to Cartersville fast enough. I had a whole new respect for the traffic on I-75. I just could not get killed now. (Since then, many have asked me why I didn't just pray to be saved right there in the car. I just couldn't. I knew God was able to but all I could think of at the time was getting back to church. Looking back now, I realize that I had to be willing to do whatever God wanted of me and that was to do the very thing I had said I would never do. That, of course, was to go down in front of a bunch of people.)

That night at church, when the invitation was given, I was shaking all over and the tears were pouring. I touched my husband's arm and said, "Go pray with me!" As we knelt and prayed he asked, "What are we praying for?" I told him that I was lost! You see.....he didn't know the conversations that had gone on in the car earlier that day. As we prayed, Brother Don came over to us and asked, "What's going on guys?" My reply was, "I'm lost!" He smiled and said, "You can take care of that right now!" As I prayed for my salvation and surrendered to God, a funny thing happened. I didn't care who saw me....who was there...or what anybody thought! God saved my soul that night and there was no doubt!

Each day I stand amazed at his wonderful grace and mercy. What peace.....what joy......what assurance! My heart resounds with the words, "Blessed Assurance...Jesus is mine!" He can be yours too, if you will humble yourself and surrender.

IS CHRIST IN YOU??
by
MIKE LARUE

"Test yourselves to see if you are in the faith. Examine yourselves. Or do you not recognize for yourselves that Jesus Christ is in you?—unless you fail the test."
II Corinthians 13:5

My testimony is one that I believe many people can relate to, especially the men of today's busy, self-centered society. It is one of self-deception, of stubbornness, and of pride. It is a testimony of what happens when a grown man gets honest with himself and looks in the mirror realizing what he truly sees. It is a testimony about making the simple clear cut choice to either accept or reject the undeniable calling of the Holy Spirit. It was so simple, but I made it so hard. My testimony proves that God's Word and His promises are true. The story is lengthy.

God has convicted me to always include the seemingly small details whenever I share it. It is unique in that it is as much about the process I went through as it is the results. You will laugh at my stubbornness and the path I took and that is okay. You may relate to much of it. You may see your own personal mirror appear as you read this story. What will you see in that mirror? I pray that God will always convict those this story reaches to be patient and to take the time to allow each small detail and the process that I went through to speak to their hearts.

I was one of those kids who grew up in church and learned about God and Jesus at an early age. It was simply a part of my life. One day, like many other teenagers in a revival service, I responded to a very moving and emotional invitation and "went down" to the altar. After all, everyone was going down. I didn't want to be left out. I responded to peer pressure and off I went. Someone met me and prayed with me, but no one really explained anything else. I had heard about "getting saved" and figured I had done what I was supposed to do. I felt better for doing what I thought was the right thing. It was a good feeling and I remember thinking I did not have to worry about that anymore. From there, off I went with life.

Next came my twenties with marriage, work, and children. Life was passing by quickly. My mid-thirties arrived before I knew it. Career, three kids, and the ritual of church on Sunday seemed to be all life was about. I was periodically going though times of trying to "be a better Christian" and "be a better person." I was a pretty good person by anyone's standards, but soon I began to realize something was missing.

That realization really hit home one week in April of 1996 at a revival at Tabernacle Baptist Church. One night during that revival the evangelist asked the question that is asked all the time, "Do you know you are going to heaven?" I had heard it a dozen times. Then the statement came that spoke directly to me. "If you have even one percent of doubt you need to know for sure tonight." Bam! This was a statement I had never heard before, but was one that really hit me head on. "If you have even one percent of doubt"... one percent is not much. I remember thinking ninety-nine percent is pretty good. So why did this statement bother me? Do you ever get "bothered" by a certain statement or question? Can you replace the word "bothered" with "convicted?" Should you?

I began to think through my life, my early experience as a teenager, and my overall spiritual situation. I left that night "bothered" but determined to think through all of this so I would not be worried anymore. That was my first mistake . . . my plan to "think through" all of this. I went home in deep contemplation. I didn't tell my wife. After all I was a grown man and didn't need anybody else's help. That was my second mistake...thinking I was strong enough to go it alone. Does this sound familiar, men? For all you baseball fans, you can substitute the word "strike" for mistake . . . it will make sense later on.

Much to my surprise, the next night we came back home from the revival and my wife sat down obviously troubled. She shared with me that she always gets these "doubts" about her salvation whenever we have these revivals. I was shocked. Darla was a preacher's kid and she had been saved when she was 14. I was blown away that she would feel this way. That night, in the first real act of courage in my life, I looked at her and said, "me too." We stared at each other in disbelief. We talked about it for a while and agreed we should talk to someone. We decided to go see Don Startup, our Minister of Music, who we had become friends with over the past year. I have got to tell you how big a step that was for me. I was too strong a man to agree to go to "counseling" for anything! What if somebody found out? Are you seeing the pride come out in this story?

We did go and meet with Don, sharing our concerns. It was so very hard to admit we were questioning our salvation. After all we were faithful church members and even sang in the choir! Don was so very helpful, but was of course unable to give us the cut and dried answer we wanted. Don quoted **II Corinthians 13:5** which says,

"Test yourselves to see if you are in the faith. Examine yourselves. Or do you not recognize for yourselves that Jesus Christ is in you?—unless you fail the test."

He also asked us if we were willing to do whatever God showed us we needed to do. We both agreed. We left that day to examine ourselves but we each took a different path.

Darla wisely chose to search her heart. I stubbornly chose to search my mind. Darla began to pray for God to show her what she needed to know.

Because she exercised faith that God would give her the answer she needed, she quickly came to the realization that she had been deceived at age 14 and had responded emotionally to the pressure of others. God spoke to her heart the very next day while she was driving up the interstate and revealed to her that she was indeed lost. That night was the last night of the revival and she came forward and was miraculously saved. Her story is an entirely different but wonderful testimony all its own. (Be sure to read it!)

I was fortunate to be a part of her marvelous transformation, but it actually confused me even more. I figured since I didn't receive some kind of quick revelation about my salvation that I was probably saved, and all those doubts were just in my mind. I foolishly continued to attempt to logically prove to myself that I was saved. This struggle went on for several miserable weeks. I prayed; I read a book on eternal security; and I thought about it constantly. One day I was reading this book feverishly when Darla came into the room and simply stated that I was not going to find my answer in a book. She told me I needed to have faith, pray, and search my heart. I blasted her and told her I had to do this my way. Big mistake…once again. I was so stubborn. Her words did have an impact on me though. I could not get away from the words "faith" and "heart;" even though, I was focused on my feelings and my own thoughts.

During this two week struggle, the words to a song we had done in choir kept coming to me over and over. The song is "It Was Enough." One of the phrases, "It was enough the blood that I shed, what more can I do" kept coming to me over and over. I kept telling myself I believed that Jesus died for my sins, but somehow it just wasn't real to me. I continued to struggle becoming more and more miserable with each passing day. During this time Darla was at the ball field one evening with our son while I was at work and shared her experience with a friend of ours who is a member at Tabernacle as well. The very next Sunday when Darla went forward to make her decision public he and his sister got saved. They had been church members for years and years. It was a special moment that God really used to soften my stubborn prideful heart. I was a total wreck at this point, but still just could not let go of my way of doing things.

The next Tuesday night we had an extra choir rehearsal for our upcoming presentation of "God with Us." The second I stepped out of the car the Holy Spirit was all over me. I had such a strong feeling of anticipation. During our rehearsal Brother Don had some choir members come up and give a testimony about how God had made a way for them during a difficult time in their lives. God used those words of testimony to utterly and completely humble me. While we were singing, "God Will Make a Way," the Holy Spirit just overwhelmed me with all the events and struggles of the last several weeks. The Holy Spirit revealed the "strikes" or opportunities I had been shown over the last two weeks. I have another whole story I could tell about how the Holy Spirit revealed to me that this special night was strike three, but for the sake of time, just know that there was no mistaking the simple clear cut choice that confronted me at that moment. Oh dear friend . . . there is no doubt that Satan was hard at work that night telling me it was not Sunday morning and that I should wait. After all, I could not disrupt the rehearsal!

Yes, at that moment I clearly recognized both the gentle drawing of the Holy Spirit and the forces of evil that had me paralyzed. But you know what? I made what had suddenly become a logical clear cut decision. The Holy Spirit stands at the door to our hearts and knocks. God created us with the special gift of choice. I had a decision to make and it was to reject or accept His calling to my heart. Time was standing still for me. I continued to resist. All of a sudden, I realized my heart was telling my mind what to do instead of my mind telling my heart what to do. It was time to follow my heart just like Darla had said. It was time to accept that it was enough, what Jesus did for me on the cross. He did the same for you. Do you know that?

The choir was still singing "God Will Make a Way." I realized he had made a way for me so I got up! I walked down to Brother Don, grabbed his arm, and pulled him off the stage. I think I really scared him! He asked what was going on? When I could finally talk I told him I had been searching for my answer and that I had found it. I told him I had been searching with my mind and not my heart but that I had finally discovered my heart was not right and that I have trusted Jesus only with my mind and not with my heart. I told him I was ready to trust him

NOW! Don, of course, did not tell me to come back on Sunday morning. He said, "You can take care of it right here if you want." I said, "yes! . . . here!" We knelt at the front pew and Don started praying something but I didn't hear it. I just remember taking over. I remember to this day what I prayed. I prayed, "Lord . . . I know I'm a sinner. Lord . . . I know You can cover my sins with Your blood and I believe that. Lord . . . I pray that You will forgive me of all my sins. Lord . . . I've trusted You with my mind and my feelings all these years, but not with my heart. I'm ready now...to trust You with my heart. Lord I give my heart to You! Thank You, Lord Jesus!" In that moment he saved me for all eternity! In that instant I saw the 38 years of my life laid out before me and washed away. What freedom I felt. I was truly and miraculously born again. I felt the Holy Spirit just flood my soul. I had been so stubborn and prideful that I almost missed heaven. Don then prayed, "Thank You, Lord, for saving Mike!" We got up and he said we should tell the choir. I was more than glad to do so. I grabbed the microphone and quickly told them what had happened. I noticed I was not the only one crying. The Holy Spirit was all over that place that night. It was simply amazing. I had a one on one encounter with the Savior and got to have 80 to 90 witnesses to the greatest moment of my life. No more doubts . . . ever again. It was awesome. I went back to the altar and just thanked the Lord for what He had done while the choir sang the final song of rehearsal. It is a moment in time I will never forget. If you do not have that special moment in time, I beg you to search your heart today.

We left church that night and drove straight to Tim Smith's house, our Education Minister, to tell him and his wife Cathy what had happened. Steve McCombs our Youth Minister and his wife Tonya lived a few houses away from Tim and Cathy. We called them to meet us there. I told them all what had just happened. The six of us gathered in a circle and both of these dear minister friends lifted up wonderful prayers of thanksgiving. I thought the roof was going to come off of that house. The Holy Spirit was still working so strongly. Both of these couples have been such a special influence on Darla, our kids, and me over the years. I just had to share this moment with them. It was truly an awesome night.

This story has been long and I hope you understand now why sharing the process in such detail is so important. Since that very day the Lord has always convicted me to emphasize the process as much as the result. I believe that is because there is a message in the process I went through that can reach some people that no other method can reach. I feel very strongly about that. In the days following my salvation, the Lord prompted me to write all of this down. I sat down one day and typed every little detail of this story out . . . tears pouring the whole time. It is 10 pages . . . single spaced. Consider yourself lucky today . . . you actually have the condensed version!

That special night was April 30th, 1996. The following weeks and months were amazing. I got up everyday feeling like I had hit a home run in the

World Series. A home run is one of the greatest and most unique achievements in all of sports. As soon as you hit it you are victorious, but the real reward doesn't come until after you cross home plate. When you hit a home run, you get to take that home run trot . . . running confidently around the bases, heading for home. During that trot, you can look over your left shoulder, savor the moment, and see what is waiting for you at home plate. Your team mates are there, just on the other side, cheering you on and waiting to greet you. If you can't view life like this, maybe you should really be examining your heart. If so, **II Corinthians 13:5** has a message for you.

Following my experience, the Lord convicted me very strongly that I had a message that the men of our church needed to hear. On October 20th, 1996 I had the opportunity to share my testimony with the church in the morning services. It was my 39th birthday and was another day I will never forget. When I finished my testimony in the last service, Brother Don felt led to give an invitation before the pastor came to deliver the message. He simply asked if there was anyone that needed Jesus, now was the time. He said we would sing one verse of "God Will Make a Way" and if no one needed to respond we would continue on with the service. Right at the end of the chorus, one person came down. We sang a second verse and another came down, then another and another. The Holy Spirit was poured out during that service in a mighty way. Forty minutes later 25 to 30 people had come forward to accept Christ. The pastor never got to preach on that day. God had another plan. To this day I am still amazed at how God can take my simple story of stubbornness and pride and use it to draw people to him like he did on that day. The gift of salvation is available to all who will choose to accept it. **Have you accepted or rejected the saving grace of Jesus Christ?** It is a question we must all answer. If your answer is "rejected", please turn to the Appendix in the back of this book for a word from Billy Graham. He would love to help you nail down your decision today!

A WORK IN PROGRESS
by
KIM LEWIS

"And I am certain that God, who began the good work within you, will continue his work until it is finally finished on the day when Christ Jesus returns."
Philippians 1:6 (NLT)

The oldest of three, I was raised in the small town of Glencoe, Alabama. My parents had us in church before we were born! Glencoe First United Methodist, my "home church," was full of wonderful people who loved me and taught me about the love of God. When I was six, I clearly remember our preacher, Bobby Ray Halbrooks, explaining the need to ask Jesus in your heart. I'm sure I had heard it before, but it seemed so plain to me at that moment. I had talked to God as long as I could remember, but I didn't want to leave any room for chance. That night,

I went home and in the darkness of my bedroom (complete with pink shag carpet), I asked Jesus to forgive my sins and to come into my heart. As much as a six year old can understand and be sincere...I was.

From an early age, I had a love for God's Word. I would lie in my bed, after my parents had turned out the lights, and read my Bible with a light-up compact mirror that I kept by the bedside. (You never know when you'll need a compact in the middle of the night.) I shared a bed with my baby sister so I always tried hard not to wake her or let my parents know I was still up. Though I had a desire to read and know God's Word, I had no real understanding of HOW it applied to my life. That lesson would come much later.

I had spent my middle school years very involved in our church youth group, choir and all the other activities a "young Christian girl" should be involved in, but I cannot say that I was living a victorious Christian life. By High School, I was plagued by stupid choices, guilt and the constant feeling that I was not really good enough. I tried to combat these feelings by self-inflicted rules and restrictions, somehow feeling like they made me more "in control" of who I was.

I don't remember how it started, but I began to limit the food I ate. I would tell myself, "You have not measured up this week, so you can only have half of a breakfast bar all day." I know it sounds crazy, but it was the way I coped with stress. Knowing that this was not right, but not really understanding why it was wrong, I played with diet pills and diet foods. Let me set the scene. I was as tall as I am now, 5'10", and barely over 100 pounds. It was NOT pretty! Eventually, that twisted system seemed pointless, plus – I was hungry. So much for self-punishment.

Eventually, I went off to college where I gained 15 pounds and surrounded myself, by the grace of God, with several other Christian girls. We all became involved in Campus Outreach and I began to be discipled by one of my sorority sisters. (They **can** be a good influence!) It was through those small group times of studying God's Word and digging deeper that I came to understand **Jeremiah 29:11,** *"For I know the plans that I have for you', declares the LORD, 'plans for welfare and not for calamity to give you a future and a hope." (NAS)* I realized, for the first time, that God's Word was meant for **me**. He had a plan, not just for mankind in general, but for me. He intended that I **know** His Word, **study** His word, **expect** His Word to speak to me, **apply** it to my life and circumstances, **believe** it for myself and **obey** what He showed me. All this was a true revelation!

I began to have a "Quiet Time" with God on a consistent basis where I studied the Word, did homework, brought Him all my concerns, fears and problems and sought Him for answers. I didn't always listen. I clearly remember one specific time when I wanted to do one thing, and God **clearly** told me to do another. It was the first time I remember thinking, "Hey, this following God thing is **not** easy! I don't know if I can say 'no' to myself and 'yes' to God."

Through a true season of wrestling it out...He won. I thank God that He did not let go of me just because I wasn't completely willing to follow. He stayed after me until I cried "Uncle!".

As college life went on, Jeff and I met; and thanks to Anne Donahoo, Gene Lewis, Kathy Howren and Steve Kennedy (yes, it took a committee) prodding him to "pop the question," **four years later**, we were finally married!

Ours had primarily been a long distance relationship. He had graduated college three years before me and was back home in White, Georgia working. After we got married, our address was Rt. 1, White, Georgia. (My friends from college thought that address was hilarious!) As wonderful as married life was, and as wonderful as people were to me, it was **not** home. I remember walking our long gravel driveway for hours, crying and feeling like someone had died. Someone had – me. Leaving my familiar home and life of 22 years proved much harder than I thought. I remember thinking, "Outside of church, I never see anyone I know. Oh yeah, I forgot...I don't know ANYBODY!" One thing I knew...I loved God and I loved my new church, Tabernacle Baptist. I laughingly told a few people that I knew God had called me to Tabernacle before I knew He had called me to marry Jeff. This was really true!

At the time, Jeff was making $400 a week and I was gainfully **un**employed. (Do the math.) I wanted to get our home established before I went to work, but obviously, I needed to hurry! After praying about where I should work, ironically, my first job was substitute teaching at the Tabernacle Learning Center, thanks to Kay Williams Covey who was a new bride herself.

Jeff and I belonged to the Young Married Sunday School Class, under the direction of Mason and Linda Brown and eventually Ed and Judy Bruce. This class was **life** to me . . . and I do mean life! They faithfully taught us the Word of God every week and it was like a spiritual B12 shot. We also connected with the other couples and truly became lifelong friends.

About that time, I started leading a ladies' Bible study with several girls from the Tabernacle singles department, thanks to the prodding of Byron Johnson. Included in our little group was Dee Tidwell, Kathy (Lombard) Gibbs and Kim (King) Poe who all put up with me as their "leader." What a joke. I was a wreck myself! But they were wonderful and patient with me and we grew a lot together.

Within a couple of years, everyone in our little Sunday School class was having their first baby – everyone except us. Tests and doctor visits revealed that there were no "real problems", but it was a "real problem" to me! Even with all the energy I had poured into school and college, all I ever really wanted was to be married and have precious children. That was fulfillment to me. . .and it wasn't happening. Months and months rocked on. The emotional pain was so intense at times that I remember thinking, "God, if you won't give me a baby, just let me die." I didn't really mean it, but at the time, it sounded like the better option.

After 18 months of invasive tests, medications and procedures, we got the news…our baby was on the way. God had answered my prayers. I was beside myself! It was the longest nine months of my life. When Macall finally arrived on May 10, 1995, I could not believe it. I had never been so happy! He was perfect to me. He had come four days before Mother's Day. **What a great Mother's Day gift!** Three years, six procedures and one surgery later, we had Parker a week before Christmas of 1998. **What a great Christmas gift!** Having been told that we would "never have any more children," you can imagine our surprise when two years later, sick with pneumonia, I discovered I was expecting Peyton. It was Dr. Lisa Sward who delivered the amazing news. Not so incidentally, he came one week before my 33rd birthday. **What a great birthday gift!**

I was truly blessed…and truly overwhelmed. I mean – really overwhelmed! (Isn't it funny how we beg God for things, then we are stressed-out when we get them?) I had three children in six years and two were in diapers. Jeff was gone a lot (can you blame him?) and I was two hours away from my mother and sister. I was not qualified for this job!! What was I thinking?? I remember making frequent calls and visits to Cindy Smith and Alison Startup (who also had three boys) for moral support. They were wonderful and I am forever grateful to them.

To make a LONG story short . . . having small children showed me just how selfish I really was. I thought I was a great person, until I became a mother. I wanted to be perfect at it, but that was impossible. It was just so hard! What was wrong with me? I loved my boys more than my own life, but the demands of two and eventually three small children, along with everything else we had going on, threw me continually into frustration and anger...and eventually to my knees. The good news is – that was exactly where God wanted me. Admitting that I could **not** do it was the first step in my very long process. You see, I had never said, "I can't." I had always said, "If I want to, I can" or, "If someone else can do it, so can I." I would then push myself to do whatever it was I had set my mind to do. For the first time in my life, I could not do what I so desperately wanted to do. The stubborn eggshell of pride was beginning to crack. I had reached the end of myself.

Through this entire process, I couldn't understand how I could love God, spend time with Him, even serve Him like I did and still be so defeated as a wife and mother. But I was. As I was reading one day about Daniel and the fiery furnace, it finally occurred to me that God refines us through fire. That was it! It was through the fire of motherhood that God was refining me. He used those constant precious "flames" to rid me of the self-life I had grown to know: self-reliance, self-righteousness, self-will and any other "self" you can think of!

In desperation, I memorized Scripture and learned more effective ways to pray. About this same time, a wise mentor taught me how to use scripture to fight my sinful flesh. I had never realized that God's word was a weapon! She taught me how to fight as scripture teaches, "according to the spirit", not the flesh.

I memorized **II Corinthians 10:3-5** *"For though we live in the world, we do not wage war as the world does. The weapons we fight with are not the weapons of the world. On the contrary, they have divine power to demolish strongholds. We demolish arguments and every pretension that sets itself up against the knowledge of God, and we take captive every thought to make it obedient to Christ."*

That was a **huge** revelation to me. I had been a Christian for years, but I had never learned how to truly fight against my flesh or the enemy. Truthfully, I had never realized that I still **had** a sinful flesh, much less an enemy. I realized I could not afford to be ignorant about these things and I willfully decided to go deeper with God. **Ephesians 6:11** tells us to *"Put on all of God's armor so that you will be able to stand firm against all strategies of the devil." (NLT)* The battle was on within and without and I had to learn quickly! (By the way, the enemy hates it when you start to deal with your own sin. He will do whatever it takes to keep you blind or believing all your problems are someone else's fault. Admission is the first step to repentance.)

Psalm 61:3 says *"For You (Lord) have been a refuge for me, a tower of strength against the **enemy**." (NASB, emphasis mine)* Truly God became a tower of strength in my life like I had never known before as I faced the enemy of my flesh and of my soul. I immersed myself in intensive Bible study and took every class I could get my hands on. (Thank you, Beth Moore!) I made ladies' retreats a priority and I sought out wise women who gave me Godly counsel and set me straight according to **Titus 2**. I guess you could say that God used my marriage and my children, the things I loved the most, to break me, so that He could rebuild me into a willing instrument, totally and completely reliant on Him. My self-reliance and perfectionistic tendencies were huge obstacles that had to go, or God could not use me.

Though the struggles are never over, I praise God that He has set me free from so many things, not the least of which were self-determination, people-pleasing and stubbornness. (Jeff would argue that I am still not free!) I am certainly **still** a "work in progress" in every area, but God is so good and so patient. I thank Him for the good work He has started in me and for the freedom I can now pass to my boys. I trust Him to continue His work in me unto completion. He has His work cut out! **Philippians 1:6** *"And I am certain that God, who began the good work within you, will continue his work until it is finally finished on the day when Christ Jesus returns." (NLT)*

THE SPIRIT INTERCEDES FOR US
by
JUDY LITTLE

"In the same way, the Spirit helps us in our weakness. We do not know what we ought to pray, but the Spirit intercedes for us with groans that words cannot express. And he who searches our hearts knows the mind of the Spirit, because the Spirit intercedes for the saints in accordance with God's will."
Romans 8:26-27

At a very young age, I learned about God and that He is always listening and watching me. I can remember as a child often crying out to God about family issues and I just knew He heard my prayers. And then I learned that God does not always answer our prayers immediately. That is where I had to pray for patience and realize that God answers in His time, not mine.

I could share many times when I was so very weak and could not possibly expect anything good to come from certain situations. But God always led me to just the right Scripture passage, just the right Christian friend, and most of all He gave me a Godly husband, who always would say in his calm, gentle way, "Now Judy, we have just got to TRUST GOD with this."

In June of 1998 my mom was diagnosed with lung cancer. I, like most daughters, just never could accept giving my mom up. I had a horror of hearing of the loss of any family member, but I knew I could never handle getting this news about my mom. My daughter had just gone off to college and I was looking forward to spending more time with Mom and doing fun things with her. I can remember one particular June morning after the news of her cancer, just lying in bed and crying out to God—"I just cannot face this day!!". But in His gentle and kind way, He let me know rather quickly that yes, Judy, you can get up and carry on through this day, because I am going to carry you through. I was out of bed before I could even think twice.

Every day as I entered my mother's back door, I just did not know what to expect, but God always gave me the strength to greet her with a smile and He always gave me encouraging words for her. We were fortunate to have her for two and a half more years after she was diagnosed and those were some FUN years that I will never forget. I had to totally depend on God through this difficult time and could have never made it through without Him.

As I was reading my daily Bible reading one day, I read **Romans 8: 26-27** about how we don't have to even utter words, because the Holy Spirit helps us in our weakness. We do not know what we ought to pray for, but the Spirit Himself intercedes for us with groans that words cannot express. And He Who searches our hearts knows the mind of the Spirit, because the Spirit intercedes for the saints in accordance with God's will. And I realized that my SWEET HEAVENLY FATHER was with me and even on those days when I just did not know what to pray for, He heard my groans and His love and concern for me is far beyond my understanding. I just thank Him and praise Him for his GOODNESS, MERCY, and GRACE and for listening to my prayers and groans and always answering in His Time and His own sweet way.

CHILD OF GOD
by
BECKY M^CCRORY

*"He predestined us to be **adopted** as his sons through Jesus Christ, in accordance with his pleasure and will"*
Ephesians 1:5 (NIV)

In 2003, our daughter, Jenny, gave her son up for adoption. The only thing we knew was that Jenny wanted <u>two</u> loving parents for her son that were Christians, and who would raise this child as a Christian. While there were many unanswered questions, we went through with the adoption.

Before we knew it, the baby was here and the papers were signed. The adoptive parents were brought into the room for the "handing over" process. Each of us said our goodbyes and reminded the adoptive parents of the commitment they had made. I walked out ahead of Jenny and made it about ten feet and just collapsed on the floor.... I know everyone must have thought I was the one having the baby because of my emotional loud cries to God. The rest of the family had escorted Jenny out the back way, and my sister-in-law stayed with me while my face was buried in the floor. As I cried to God, I begged for His mercy and His guidance to look after our "Alex" through his life.

It was at that moment that my life flashed before my eyes and I realized what a lousy mother I had been. I begged God to come back to my heart and into my life so I could help put my emotionally torn apart family back together and to give me the strength for the days ahead. Because I was so ashamed, I couldn't even hold my head up. I was trying so hard to turn everything over to God at that time, but realized that I needed Him in my heart before I could do any of that. After 10 minutes being sprawled out in the hallway, my sister-in-law got me up and took me home. I was a new person.

Several weeks after that, Jennie told me that she wanted to start going to church. I said "OK, that is a great idea. Do you have any idea where you want to go?" She said, "Yes, Tabernacle". My heart just sank because I knew the purpose was not to go to church, but to look for the adoptive parents who also attended there and for a chance to get a glimpse of her son. After I spoke with my sister-in-law and our family friends who had been through all this, they said, "Take her. You might be surprised".

We went in the church on a Wednesday or Sunday night, and Jenny waited until after the service and went up to Dr. Hattaway and began to cry. She told him she wanted to go to church and become a Christian. He put his arms around her right there, prayed with her, and then he told her that he knew of a Sunday School class that would be good for her. It was the one his wife, Sonny Hattaway, taught.

The next Sunday morning, we got dressed and took off to Sunday School, and you can just imagine how I felt, the hair on the back of my head was standing straight out, because I knew her intentions. When we got inside, I was asking about a class for me. Jenny looked at me and said, "No, I need you to go with me". I tried to explain that I was not in my 20's, or even my 30's and I would feel out of place and they may not want some old woman in a class like this. But it was that or nothing, so we went upstairs together.

When we walked in this room, I cannot remember ever feeling the overwhelming power of God's spirit on me like I felt it that day. When we sat down, I kept looking around because I was sure that Jesus was sitting in full presence to me or Jenny. We introduced ourselves and this time, I was the shy one. Jenny was going to unload her whole story on them, but Sonny directed it so well. The other people in the class just got up and hugged her and me right then. They gave us Sunday School books and Jenny volunteered to read some of the passages they were going through. I can't find the correct words, but it was just beyond amazing. They didn't just talk to Jenny, they talked to me like I was in my 20's or 30's. I was uncomfortable with my dress and ashamed of what Jenny had worn, but it took less than 30 seconds for that feeling to go away. All that was there was love, love, love.

They begged us to come back... and I said we would. We went into the worship center, and we moved at least 6 times so Jenny might be able to "see the adoptive parents", but she didn't. When we went to leave, she said she wouldn't go back because she didn't see them, and I just said in my nicest voice, "Well maybe they just weren't there today, but wasn't that Sunday School class just amazing?" She said, "I felt so good in there. They didn't judge me or make me feel stupid... weren't they nice?" I agreed and said we should try to come back next Sunday which we did. We went for six weeks to Sunday School and church looking like little rats moving around from service to service. To say the least, it was embarrassing. But I sure was enjoying it. And by this time, I was becoming so attached, I didn't want to leave the class or the church! I was so humbled and overwhelmed by the services, I couldn't stay away. Jenny started driving herself and by this time, I had gotten my sister-in-law to come to Sunday School. She said she just hated big churches, but she would go for Jenny's sake. So, here was another one... too old to be in Sonny's class, but all I asked her to do was to try it. Guess what, she did. There was such a "mismatch" of all kinds of people in this class, it didn't matter who you were or what you were.... you just fit in!

Much has happened in our lives since that time, but I thank God that He led us to Tabernacle Baptist church. More than that, I praise Him that through the painful adoption of my own grandson, God showed me His great love for me, my daughter, and my entire family. Not only are Jenny and I active at church now, but so is my sister and husband...and hopefully in the near future, my son. He used that very difficult time to draw us back to Him and change our lives. For that, I am forever grateful.

LET YOUR WILL BE DONE
by
SUSAN MAY

"Yet not as I will, but as you will."
Matthew 26:39b

"Dear God, what do I ask for? Do I want Nick to live or for you to let him die peacefully? Help me. I don't know. Please let Your will be done."

In April of 1989, I poured my heart out to God like I had never done before. At no other time in my life had I ever sincerely prayed "Your will be done" and meant it. Before I had always had the answer I wanted in mind. Nick, our new baby boy, had just been diagnosed with a life threatening heart birth defect and was to have surgery in three days with a less than fifty/fifty chance to survive..

Would the right thing be to pray for Nick to live? He was the youngest of our four children, the oldest having just turned five. Nick was a baby and the other children did not know him as a real member of our family. A newborn, I thought, would be easier to let go of than a child who became an integral part of our everyday life.

Andy and I were told that if Nick made it through this surgery alive there would be others to follow when he was older. If he died during one of those how would we ever explain his death to his brothers and sister? It would be much more difficult to lose him at four, ten, or seventeen years of age. But I could not bring myself to pray for him to die. I loved him.

As I talked to God I knew he was the only one who had the answers to my questions. Only He knew what was in the future. That night I handed my fears over to Him, asking for His will and not mine. A total sense of peace entered me. I knew then that God would be there for me and my family no matter what happened to Nick.

As the day of the surgery arrived, I knew Nick was completely in God's hands. I had given Nick over to His care. Nick came through the first surgery with flying colors, went on to have two additional heart surgeries and received a heart transplant all before the age of two.

Eighteen years later, I know it was God's will that Nick live because I have a tall, strong, and loving young man at my house.

"Dear God, Thank you for holding Nick in the palm of your hand. That's where I am happy to have him."

MOLLY BETH'S STORY
by
JULIE MITCHELL

"But my God shall supply all your needs according to his riches in glory by Christ Jesus."
Philippians 4:19

God has blessed my family in so many ways over the years. When Jimmy and I realized that we could not have children we decided we would try to adopt. God in His awesome timing brought Haley and Jeremiah into our lives. We thought that our family was complete, but God had other plans in store for us. In February, 2005, God decided to change my family's life forever. After 18 years of marriage, we were totally shocked to learn that I was expecting. I could not even imagine what was in store for us over the next two years. Even though we were very excited about the arrival of our baby, we were also nervous.

The months went by quickly, and on October 2, 2005, Molly Elizabeth Mitchell was born. She was five weeks early but weighed 5 lbs and everything seemed to be fine. When we were released from the hospital three days later, we thought we were bringing home a small, but healthy, baby girl. The day after we came home from the hospital we went for her first checkup. When her doctor listened to her heart she stated that she could hear a hole in her heart. The doctor decided to send us to a cardiologist that day. While at the office visit Molly Beth became hungry, so I started feeding her. Then, she started turning blue. The doctor immediately sent for an ambulance to pick her up and take her to Egleston Children's Hospital.

This horrible day was the first of a 19 day stay at the children's hospital. Over the next two and a half weeks, Molly Beth went through numerous tests and studies and was seen by an army of doctors. We were told that the problem with her heart would have to be repaired, and the doctors also believed that she had a genetic disorder. Jimmy and I both felt like someone had knocked the breath out of us every time we were told something new. The verse that I kept repeating was **Philippians 4:6**, *"Be anxious for nothing but in everything, by prayer and supplication with thanksgiving, let your requests be made known unto God."* I kept thanking God for the simple fact that He had allowed Molly Beth to be born.

God started opening up doors almost immediately. The second day of Molly Beth's stay in the hospital, we were able to obtain a room at the Ronald

McDonald House. This was an answer to prayer since we were over 50 miles from home, and I was only a week out from a Cesarean section. The staff at the hospital had already informed us that it was rare to be able to get in the Ronald McDonald House, since it was usually a long wait. After about seven days in the cardiac intensive care unit, Molly Beth was moved to the floor. This was another answer to prayer, but our joy was short-lived as she was moved to the Neonatal Intensive Care Unit to allow closer monitoring.

The test results started coming in, and the doctors told us that along with the hole in her heart, Molly Beth also had a grade IV bladder reflux, stomach reflux, calcium deficiency and an immune dysfunction. The other problem was that she could not eat by mouth which resulted in her having a feeding tube and numerous monitors. My heart's desire was to be able to hold my new born baby, but that was an obstacle with all of her wires. By this time I was so tired, and my hormones were still adjusting to the birth. My emotions were out of hand. Any time I spoke with family or friends I asked them to pray and to stand in the gap for me. I was at the point that I couldn't even pray.

Finally, after 19 days, we were told we could take our precious daughter home. Jimmy and I were excited but very nervous. There was so much medical information we had to learn before we could come home. We had to learn how to insert an NG tube (feeding tube), how to administer and measure eleven medications into that tube, and how to run an apnea monitor. This was so overwhelming that I asked God for a peace that only He could give me and to help me remember everything I had to do for my daughter. In **Philippians 4:19** it says *"But my God shall supply all your needs according to His riches in glory by Christ Jesus."*

The first day home went fair and was filled with family members welcoming us home. But again this good time was short lived.

That night Molly Beth's apnea monitor went off 19 times. However, every time we picked her up and turned on the light, she was pink, so we thought everything was okay. The next day we took her to her pediatrician for a follow up visit from being in the hospital. The doctor felt that the monitor was malfunctioning because Molly Beth was not turning blue. We returned home, and a couple of hours later the monitor went off again. However, this time when we reached her she was a gray color, and we knew something was wrong. Jimmy and I put her in the car and started driving to Atlanta. At this point her color had gotten much better, and she had turned pink again. We felt that we could make it back to Egleston Children's Hospital.

While on the road I called her pediatrician and left her a message telling her we were on our way back to Egleston. God was watching over us because a few minutes later the doctor returned our call and told us to stop at the Children's Urgent Care facility in Kennesaw. The doctor stayed on the phone with me until we arrived, and the doctors at the facility immediately called the Life Flight Helicopter which air lifted Molly Beth to Scottish Rite Children's Hospital. We asked that she be taken back to the other hospital, but they did not have room for her. At this point we did not realize how much this was a blessing in disguise. When we arrived at the hospital Molly Beth was put in the intensive care unit. The head doctor came out to talk with us, and stated that Molly Beth's blood had an infection in it but at that time they did not know why. The next day we were told that she had a kidney infection that had set up e coli in her blood stream.

We knew God had given Molly Beth to us for a reason, but we could not understand why she was having to endure all of these problems. I realized during this time that I had to rely on God for everything, and I believe we all forget to do that when everything is rocking along okay. We forget to stop and praise Him for the little things in life as well as the big things. Jimmy and I became closer during this time since we had to rely on each other for so much. We had to make sure that one of us was always at the hospital and that our other two children were being cared for. We could not have done this without the support of our family, friends and our wonderful church.

During this 13 day hospital stay, Molly Beth was taken off a lot of her medications including all the heart medication she had been on. Even though she still had the hole in her heart, it had made some changes. We were now told that they would monitor her heart but would hold off on surgery . This was big news for us but that high would quickly be taken away. The genetics doctor visited us during our stay with the test results. She informed us that Molly Beth had a chromosomal abnormality with an unbalanced 9P/20P translocation. This meant that her number 9 chromosome and her number 20 chromosome tips had broken off and changed places. The only thing she could tell us was that there was only one other child in their genetic data base that had something similar to Molly Beth's disorder. The doctor said it would be hard to compare her with the other patient because his breaks were more severe. In her exact words, Molly Beth's prognosis was unknown. The doctor could not tell us if she would ever sit up, walk, talk or eat by mouth. Even though we were shocked at her prognosis, we knew that we still loved our daughter dearly, and we would do everything possible to take care of her, love her and teach her everything possible. (Her prognosis may be unknown to the doctors, but I know that God has it all under control!)

On November 6, 2005 we brought our beautiful daughter home. Since that time we have had numerous doctors visits and continue to have different tests run. Molly Beth has only had one surgery and that was to put in a more permanent feeding tube. It has been a very trying time, and since that day we have had our lows, but we have also had great triumphs. Molly Beth receives occupational therapy, physical therapy, speech therapy and aquatics. She has accomplished the task of sitting up by herself, says "bye-bye" and "da da" and can also eat a little yogurt by mouth. Even though she has had set backs from a condition that has made her have severally brittle bones resulting in five broken bones since birth, I feel sure that walking is in the near future. Molly Beth endures so much everyday from her therapies, eating problems and numerous doctors visits, but she still has the sweetest personality and smile. Everyone that meets her never forgets her smile.

In **Matthew 11:28**, Jesus says *"Come unto me, all ye that labor and are heavy laden, and I will give you rest."* The past two years have been a trying time for our family, but God has brought us through and continues to show us everyday His miraculous power.

EMERGENCY 911
by
HOLLY MUNTZ

"But in my distress I cried out to the Lord; yes, I cried to my God for help. He heard me from his sanctuary; my cry reached his ears"
II Samuel 22:7 (MSG)

When I was a young girl around eight or nine years of age, my brother and sister and I were outside playing in our yard. We had several large pine trees that reached about 50 feet in the air. One Sunday afternoon, we were out in the yard playing and my older brother, who was 12 at the time, got aggravated with us and decided to climb one of the pine trees. My sister and I continued to play not noticing that our brother had disappeared. About 10 to 20 minutes had passed and we heard our brother scream out. We didn't see him anywhere. Then my sister looked up in the tree and saw him dangling from a few branches, which he was laying on face up. I ran in the house to get my father, who did not even stop to put his shoes on.

We ran out the door and my father climbed the tree trying to keep my brother from falling 50 feet to the ground. We called 911 and the fire department. It seemed like forever had passed. Our whole neighborhood heard us screaming and came to our side. The fire department sent a truck that did not have a bucket so they had to get a truck that was able to reach over 50 feet in the air. A few hours had passed and my father's feet were close to giving out. When they finally got my brother and father down it was getting dark. They found my brothers shoe 20 feet away and his pants had a hole burned through the side. The ambulance took him to the hospital. I can remember praying so hard for my brother's life to be spared.

The whole neighborhood was at our home watching the other six of us as my mother and father were at the hospital caring for my brother. About a year prior to that day, Georgia Power had cut out the top of the trees to make way for power lines. The top of those trees were not far at all from the lines. My brother had many skin graphs done to repair the burns to his skin. I remember most of all my mother telling me if my brother had grabbed the lines with his other hand, that the volts would have gone straight through his heart and killed him instantly. My mother also reminded me later in life, that while he was in the hospital, I wrote my brother a letter and in so many words, that I wish that I was a boy so that he would have a brother. You see he was an only boy with six sisters.

Today my brother is 40 years old with 3 beautiful children and a lovely wife. We don't talk of the accident often, but I know that there are times when my family is together that my brother has this look in his eyes that he is so very glad to be alive.

I know that my brother is alive today because of God's grace and our faith in Him. My God is so good.

FULLY HIS
by
KATHY OLIVET

"May you experience the love of Christ, though it is too great to understand fully. Then you will be made complete with all the fullness of life and power that comes from God".
Ephesians 3:19

I was born in Cedartown, GA in 1948. However, my first home was Esom Hill, GA, a tiny community that had a long rectangular building that was the General store and post office…and little else. The closest church was Shiloh Baptist. This, I'm sure, was the first church I attended. And even though my family moved a lot, my earliest memories of Sunday School and Vacation Bible School were at that little country church.

My Grandpa and Grandma Henderson lived on a farm in Eson Hill. In the living room of the big, old, gray-wood farmhouse was a coffee table. On that coffee table was the family Bible. In the center of that Bible were blue pages with black illustrations and bluish-white highlights. These pages told about the life of Jesus.

I was fascinated by the blue pages. Every visit to Grandma's and Grandpa's eventually found me at the coffee table, turning the pages slowly as I studied them. It wasn't until my grandparents died that I learned that those "visits" to the coffee table had not gone unnoticed. That Bible is now mine...and yes, I still look at those blue pages.

When I was a sophomore in High School, I tried to be an atheist. That lasted 2 days. After that, I didn't thing much about religion. There was no church life. It wasn't until I was married and had a child of my own that God chose to get my attention.

I was watching TV and a movie came on, "A Man Called Peter"/ Peter Marshall was a Scottish born minister who became the chaplain of the United States Senate in 1947. The movie was a true story about Peter's walk with "the Chief", as he referred to God.

At one point in the movie, Peter began a sermon describing the Jesus he knew and served. He wasn't "the pale, anemic, namby-pamby Jesus...the gentle Jesus, meek and mild, but the Christ of the Gospels, striding up and down the dusty miles of Palestine, sun-tanned, bronzed and fearless. The knuckles big in His carpenter hands. The Christ that upset the money lenders. The Christ who loved people – all kinds of people. But particularly red-blooded folk. For He Himself was red-blooded..."

Until that moment, I had thought of Jesus as some ethereal being, floating somewhere above the clouds...the mysterious Jesus of the blue pages.

The seed was planted yes, but germination would not take place for a number of years. It wasn't until 1974 that I returned to the church of my childhood. It was there that I accepted Jesus as my Lord and Savior. I was baptized in a tiny pond and so began my journey as a servant of Jesus.

During this time I worked at Goodyear Mills in Rockmart, Georgia. One day I stood at the window and a thought came to me, "You need to call Delores." Delores was my cousin, but she was more like a sister. I was startled at this sudden thought and dismissed it. Three days later, I found out that Delores had been in a terrible car accident about the time I had the thought. She was in a coma and did wake up a few days later, but it was very serious.

Through that incident, I learned 2 important lessons: **1**. Listen for God's message and **2**. When He tells you to do something...do it!

It was a few years later before I gave everything to God...my children, my family, my situation...everything. Most importantly, I FULLY gave Him my will and totally accepted His will for my life...no mater what that entailed.

In closing my story, I would like to share a prayer that sums up my goal as a servant of the Lord Jesus. This prayer is attributed to St. Francis...

Lord, make us instruments of your peace.
Where there is hatred, let us sow love,
Where there is injury, pardon,
Where there is discord, union,
Where there is doubt, faith,
Where there is despair, hope,
Where there is darkness, light,
Where there is sadness, joy.

Grant that we may not so much seek to be consoled,
as to console,
Be understood as to understand,
Be loved as to love.
For it is in giving that we receive,
It is in pardoning that we are pardoned
And it is in dying that we are born to eternal life.
Amen

THE LORD'S LOVE
by
CHRIS OVERVOLD

"For great is your love toward me; you have delivered me from the depths of the grave."
Psalms 86:13

My eyes drifted away from the pulpit to the words on the wall behind, " *I know that my Redeemer liveth*" **Job 19:25 (KJV)** then down to my family below the rear choir loft where I was seated. Dad went to work each morning, mom stayed home (we were a one car family). My brother, sister and I enjoyed running in the fields and woods next to our suburban house when we weren't doing something less important, like going to school. My personal calendar began with the opening of duck hunting season, then on to pheasants, snow skiing, and fishing to round the year off. Not untypical of a baby boomer growing up in Minnesota during the "Andy Griffith" era. Everything was "guuu-uhd".

Our Missouri Synod Lutheran Church held fast to the teachings of scripture. For me, the inevitable hard questions of youth, "This is what I have been told is true, now why should I believe it's true?", began to surface in my Sunday School class – particularly over evolution. I was being inundated daily in school with "facts" that seemed to contradict the bible, and science was my favorite subject!

It was a turning point. Rather than bearing the yoke in youth (**Lamentations 3:27-30**), I chose the world's way. By the time I got back from Vietnam, I was an alcoholic. I managed to get through college, marry and hold down a good job in medical sales, but being fueled on pride, fear, and alcohol eventually took its toll.

My marriage ended 12 years after it had begun, the career went on for a few more. I was living in a vacation home in northern Minnesota. I had built it mostly on my own over the previous 7 years. It was a labor of love – I cleared the land, picked out the logs I wanted for the house and laid them up, planted pasture, built a small barn, fitted stone for the steps and walk – everything I had dreamed about doing when I was young. The location on a small pond between 2 large unpopulated lakes was idyllic. This was going to be the answer to all the years of running – peace, beauty and no mortgage.

As I sank deeper into alcoholism and depression, this dream cottage out of a Thomas Kinkade painting began to look more like a coffin. I finally sold it. Just weeks later I woke up in jail 150 miles from where I lived, bleeding and broken.

There may be no greater agony for family and friends than watching someone they love on a death march. When I was finally ready, help came from every direction. Years of daily prayers were coming to fruition – especially those of my family. The Lord led us to an outpatient treatment center that was staffed exclusively by Christians – something that was unheard of in this area. It was there during a group session that I turned to my counselor and said, "Without God, I'm a dead man".

A man named Ed had been patiently counseling me, answering questions and opening up scriptures. He and his wife, Marcie, opened their house to a number of us each Friday evening. I can still feel the cool breezes coming through the screens, smell the fresh hot coffee, hear the laughter and see the tears. My appetite for scripture became voracious.

The first book I read was Job (as the result of hearing a man I respected quote from it on National Public Radio of all places – God's hand at work again!). In **Job 36 verses 8-15**, the words "lived" in a way I had never experienced before. After He and I got a few things straight, (even His words of reproof are glorious and full of love) God, through His people, led me into a personal relationship with His son, Jesus (**John 6:44,65**).

That was 15 years ago and the blessings continue to flow! He brought a wonderful lady into my life. Judy is truly a Proverbs 31 wife! I also have two wonderful step-daughters – Anna and Rebekah. He continues to give me the greatest blessing of all, revealing Himself to me through the Word, through prayer, through His people and through serving Him in our church and in community missions. I look forward to the day when I (we) can fall down at His feet, worship, cast our crowns before Him and experience joy complete!

SECURE IN MY SALVATION
by
SHEILA PARKER

"I give them eternal life, and they shall never perish; no one can snatch them out of my hand."
John 10:28

My Aunt Edith, who raised me, was a faithful servant of God. Each time the doors of the church were opened – we were there! Sometimes we went to church when no one else was there to clean, run off bulletins, etc. She was always working for the Lord. So, I guess on some level, even as a small child, I knew that God was very important in our life as a family.

I can't tell you the date or a time, but one day at church I was actually listening to the pastor. I felt this need inside of me that I had never felt before. I was only six years old. I did not know what to do, so I did nothing. Later that day, my Aunt asked me if something was wrong. I told her I felt that I should have talked to the pastor. She got out her Bible and simply, carefully read and explained the plan of salvation to me. I don't know if we prayed, or if she prayed for God to guide me, but that night at church I went forward. I told the pastor I needed Jesus to come into my heart.

As I grew up, and especially during the teen years, I started doubting my salvation. Because I had been so young, I thought that maybe I really didn't know what I was doing. I prayed, worried and sought advice until I almost drove myself crazy. Finally, one day, I prayed for peace. I asked the Lord that if I had not been saved to please show me. I can't say that I never doubted again, but I knew that accepting Christ was by faith.

Years later when my son Luke was around the same age as I had been, he began asking the same questions. I took him to visit my Aunt Edith. She did with him as she had done with me years earlier; she got out her Bible and read, explained so he could understand, and prayed. My beautiful son was saved.

Aunt Edith went to be with the Lord several years ago, but what a testimony she was to me and to our family. Her legacy will live on through all the people she reached for Christ.

Accepting Christ does not mean that we become perfect people. I have failed many times and have made countless mistakes. The difference – God loves and forgives us if we truly ask His forgiveness. He will restore our peace. Each day is a journey, some better than others. With Jesus in my life, I have a security that nothing in this world could give me.

Praise God from whom all blessings flow!

GOD IS GOOD
by
LIBBY BEASLEY-PERDUE

"For the Lord God is a sun and shield; the Lord bestows favor and honor; no good thing does he withhold from those whose walk is blameless."
Psalm 84:11

In August 2003 my husband of 22 years died of cancer. This was a very difficult time. We were already planning to move to Cartersville to be near our youngest daughter, so I moved to Cartersville by myself. After two months of intense grieving, I came to Tabernacle to visit. Being a seminary graduate, I wanted a pastor who preached the Word. Dr. Hattaway filled the bill.

I started attending the "Single Again" class. The ladies of the class lifted me up when I felt like a broken person. God had led me to a church that was perfect for my situation. As I was strengthened, the Lord opened the door for me to once again teach a class. The Lord also brought a Christian man into my life from the "Singles Again" class. We've been married for over two years now.

I feel the Lord broke me to rebuild me for His specific plans. I am stronger now that I have learned, like never before, that the Lord is my strength and hope. With the knowledge of His loving care from firsthand experience, I know I can face tomorrow with confidence no matter what life throws my way.

THE POHL FAMILY TESTIMONY (JIM, NANCY and DAN)
by
NANCY POHL

"And this is the testimony: God has given us eternal life, and this life is in His Son. He who has the Son has life; he who does not have the Son of God does not have life".
I John 5:11&12

The testimony I would like to share focuses on who God has shown Himself to be at different stages of our lives. Regardless of what God does, He is worthy of praise because of who He is (**1 Chronicles 16:25; 1 Chronicles 29:10-13**).

First, I will testify that God is Savior (**Isaiah 43:1,3; Ephesians 2:8; 1 Timothy 4:9-10; 1 John 4:13-16**). All three of us – Jim, Dan, and I have trusted in Jesus Christ as Savior, but each of us were saved in different ways. This shows me that God is personal **(Psalm 139; Isaiah 49:16; Matthew 10:30-31; John 10:3).**

I was saved as an adult and experienced God's forgiveness, grace, and unconditional love **(Numbers 14:18; Psalm 18:16-19; Psalm 40:1-3; Psalm 103:11-12).** Jim was saved at the age of 13 when the Holy Spirit showed him his need for a Savior apart from personal goodness and church attendance **(Romans 5:1, 6-8; Romans 6; Romans 10:9-10; Ephesians 2:8-9).** Dan's heart was moved by the Holy Spirit at the young age of four **(2 Timothy 3:14-15).**

God works in ways we don't always see. He orchestrates events and situations to accomplish His will in the world. If you know God, you know there is no such thing as an accident, luck, chance or coincidence. God is purposeful and no one can stop or thwart His plans **(Deuteronomy 32:4; Job 36:5; Job 42:2; Psalm 33:11; Psalm 57:2; Psalm 121:1-8; Psalm 134:6; Psalm 139:16)**

We have witnessed this characteristic of God in how Jim and I met and were married, in our move to Georgia, and in the way He has directed the path of Dan's life (college, friends, activities, ministry, etc.). We have learned that God's will is made evident as you walk forward in faith **(Genesis 12:1,4a; Psalm 91:1-13; Hebrews 11:8).**

If God were not the foundation of our marriage and family there were times when we would have crumbled **(Psalm 127:1; Ecclesiastes 4:12; Isaiah**

28:16; Matthew 7:24-27), but God has shown Himself to be trustworthy and true **(2 Samuel 7:28; Psalm 119:138)**. Our circumstances change all the time, but God remains the same; unchanging throughout eternity **(Psalm 48:18; Psalm 102:27; Malachi 3:6)**

When God called me to leave my career to become a stay at home mom, He filled my life with purpose and gave me work to do for Him **(Psalm 90:17; Habakkuk 3:19; Ephesians 2:10)**. God gave me satisfaction beyond what the world could offer in money, possessions, position and accomplishments **(Psalm 90:14; Psalm 103:2-5; Psalm 145:16; Luke 12:15)**. I discovered that His Word and God, Himself, are treasures worth seeking **(Ecclesiastes 5:10; Matthew 6:19-21; Colossians 2:2-3; Colossians 3:1**-4) and that when I seek God and His righteousness then what I need will be provided **(Matthew 6:33)**. The rewards I receive from God are eternal **(Matthew 16:27; Ephesians 6:8; Colossians 3:23-24; Hebrews 11:26; Revelation 22:12)**.

About two years after we moved to Georgia from Michigan, Jim's job was eliminated and he was out of work for several months. God proved Himself faithful. He never left us nor forsook us **(Psalm 9:10; Psalm 16:5-6; Psalm 68:19; Romans 8:35-39)**. God used His people to minister to us, encourage us **(Romans 12:4-8,13)** and pray for us. God provided for us in ways we couldn't explain or expect. God, Himself, ministered to us during this time through His Presence and His peace **(Psalm 29:11; Psalm**

37:4; Psalm 139:7-10; John 14:27; Romans 8:26-27,34; Philippians 4:6-7)

Twelve years ago, God led us to take guardianship of a 16 year old girl **(Psalm 68:6a)**. Through this experience we learned that God is all-powerful. He taught us the mighty power of His spoken word **(Ephesians 6:17; Hebrews 4:12)**, the power of prayer **(2 Kings 6:16-17; Romans 8:26-27; Ephesians 6:18)**, His power and dominion over evil **(Matthew 8:16; Matthew 17:18; Ephesians 6:10-18)** and His power to transform lives **(Ephesians 4:22-24; 2 Corinthians 3:18; 2 Corinthians 5:17)**.

God has given us so much more than we could ever hope for. He takes away what we don't need or what hinders our relationship with Him. He, alone, knows what's best for us **(Exodus 34:6-7; 1 Chronicles 29:14; Job 23:10; Psalm 5:12; Psalm 119:71-72; Psalm 139; Matthew 7:11; Philippians 4:12-13, 19)**.

As we raised our son, God gave us wisdom beyond our ability **(Psalm 90:12; James 1:5)**, answered prayers according to His will **(1 John 5:14)**, and faith to leave Dan in His hands, trusting Him to complete the work He has started **(Psalm 138:8; Ephesians 2:10; Philippians 1:6)**.

Through the loss of loved ones, God has shown us that He understands our pain **(Psalm 116:15; Hebrews 4:15)**. God gave His own beloved Son **(John 3:16; Romans 8:32)**. He is close to the brokenhearted **(Psalm 34:18; Psalm 147:3)** and He gives hope to the hopeless **(Psalm 62:5; 2 Thessalonians 2:16-17; Hebrews 6:17-20)**

God has been our defender (**Exodus 14:14; Deuteronomy 31:6;**), strength, shield, and reward (**Genesis 15:1; Exodus 15:2; 2 Samuel 22:31; 1 Chronicles 16:11**) because God is for us, who can be against us (**Micah 7:8-10; Romans 8:28-31; Hebrews 13:5-6**).

When we haven't known what to do or where to go, God has been our light and our guide. He hems us in on all sides and shows us the way to go (**2 Samuel 22:29; 2 Chronicles 14:11; 2 Chronicles 20:12; Psalm 4:6; Psalm 18:28-29,36; Psalm 32:8; Psalm 43:3; Psalm 48:14**) God is all-sufficient and He, alone, gives meaning and purpose to our lives. Apart from Him, we can do nothing (**John 15:1-8; 2 Corinthians 12:9**).

1 John 5:11-12 says, "And this is the testimony: God has given us eternal life, and this life is in His Son. He who has the Son has life; he who does not have the Son of God does not have life". As a family, our lives are in the Son. We praise God for all He has done and will continue to do in and through us. But we praise Him most, not for what He has done, but for who He is. He is worthy of all honor, glory and worship.

GOD WORKS IN MYSTERIOUS WAYS
by
CHARLES PUCKETT

"He is the Rock, his works are perfect, and all his ways are just. A faithful God who does no wrong, upright and just is he."
Deuteronomy 32:4

In 1957 I was stationed in Austin, Texas at Bergristom Air Force Base and I was engaged to a girl from Texas. In 1958 I had a dream about the girl that I was supposed to marry. It turned out NOT to be the girl I was engaged to. The girl from Texas and I broke our engagement because she wanted to stay in Texas. So, I came home to Cartersville, Georgia in August of 1958.

There were no jobs in Cartersville. We were told that a guy from McDonnell Aircraft Co. in St. Louis was in Atlanta and that he was hiring flight line mechanics. Me and my 2 buddies traveled to Atlanta. We had on T-shirts and blue jeans. The man we met with when we got down there was dressed in a three piece suit. He looked at us like, "I do not want anything to do with these three rednecks." So, I asked him if he was interested in hiring someone with two years experience with 101 Voodo Aircraft. He asked us when we wanted to start work! We told him, the 25th of September.

We traveled to St. Louis and started to work. I was on day shift. We went to a small drive-in restaurant in St. Charles, Missouri. It was around November, 1958. I walked in the restaurant and saw this girl behind the counter. I had to do a double-take because she was the same person I saw in my dream! We started to date and on April 18, 1959 we were married. I came back home in February of 1964 with a beautiful wife and 2 beautiful daughters. (We have now been married for 48 years.)

I got a job right away with Lockheed Aircraft Co. and we did work on C130s and C5As. (Once we went to Edwards Airforce Base to work on C5As.) I was put in charge of transportation and worked 2nd shift. The guys that rode with me on Friday nights wanted to go to bars, but I would go back to our work trailer. One Saturday morning, there was a knock at my door. The "guys" had brought me a date. I told the little lady that I was married and that I did not cheat on my wife.

In August of 1970, we were working one Saturday night when a C5A blew up. I went under it looking for my buddy. All of a sudden, I realized God was telling me that I needed to get out from under the aircraft or I would be killed. I came out from under the aircraft and found my buddy....he was under the #3 engine and he was dead. I believe with all my heart that if I had not been faithful to my wife, I would not be here today and I would not have a son to carry on my name. Nor would I be here for my family. I truly believe you can make or break your destiny by not being faithful. I give thanks to God for HIS faithfulness to me!

I HAVE NEVER WALKED ALONE
by
LYDIA QUILLEN

"But as for me, it is good to be near God. I have made the Sovereign LORD my refuge; I will tell of all your deeds."
Psalm 73:28

As a child I was taught Christian truths, but it was not until I became a young wife and mother that I gave my life to the Lord. In 1966 I was baptized and became a member of a Baptist church in Mobile, Alabama, where my husband was attending the University of South Alabama studying for a degree in electrical engineering.

In 1972 we joined the Mormon Church, where we were active members for over 20 years. Through this time, I continued to have a sense of God's presence in my life and together, we shared in many faith exercising experiences.

The most challenging occurred in 1989. In the early morning of March 22, I received the dreaded phone call that my childhood sweetheart and husband of 28 years had been killed in a plane crash. At this time he had been flying for 22 years as a private commercial-rated pilot. He was 44 years of age and God had blessed us with two lovely daughters and two grandchildren. My world as I had known it had been shattered.

From the moment I was told he had died, there was a sense of emotional and physical strength I had never experienced before. I knew I was in the arms of my loving Heavenly Father and Savior. He walked me through the deep valley of despair and sorrow.

The Lord continued to direct my path that led me to my second husband, Paul Quillen, in 1991. Amazingly, he was another nerd and electrical engineer! He brought into my family four beautiful daughters. Paul and I have had our share of faith testing experiences as well.

In 1997 we suddenly and tragically lost Paul's second daughter, Jamie Ann, at 19 years of age in an automobile accident. It's one thing to lose a spouse, and another to lose a child at such a young age. Once again, we were lifted up in the arms of our Savior receiving comfort and strength to face our life without her. She will always be with us; her memory will forever live on.

It was around this time we had begun to question the Mormon religion. I had been a member for 22 years, and Paul for 27. In 1998 we were delivered from its bondage.

In December 2003 Paul had a major heart attack, a 99% blockage in the aorta, also known as "the widow maker." As I rushed him to the Cartersville Medical Center, I felt that I was losing him. He said he was "ready" and I said I was not! It was one of those "been there, done that, don't want to do it again" moments. Paul was transported to Redmond in Rome, Georgia for emergency surgery. The 30+ miles by car for me seemed like an eternity. I did not think I would see him alive again, especially since I arrived before the ambulance. I did not receive the "peace that passes all understanding" until the ambulance arrived and I saw one of the medics, who is a dear Christian friend. He told me that they had lost Paul, but it simply was not his time. I began to give thanks and praise for answered prayer, once again. As Paul returned from surgery, he said he was ready but that his job here was not finished. And of course, I agreed wholeheartedly.

In August 2004 the Lord called my identical twin sister home. Leona had a liver transplant 15 years earlier; however, she still suffered from multiple health problems. She had a true testimony of God's grace and mercy as she continually praised the Lord through her ailments. Losing her was like losing a limb – I'm still stumbling around, but she will always be with me as we were inseparable.

Now, rather than looking at each challenge as a test, we view them as "stepping stones" toward maturing as a Child of God. Every morning we pray to be in God's will, thanking Him for each and every day. *"I will bless the Lord at all times; praise shall continually be in my mouth"* ***(Psalm 34:1).***

We are truly blessed! We have six grandsons, four granddaughter, two great grandchildren, and one daughter yet to start her family. We are looking forward to the future. This November (2007) will be two years as members of Tabernacle Baptist Church. We love and appreciate our pastor and all those that serve with him.

NO CHALLENGE HE CAN'T HANDLE
by
DAWN ROCKEY

"Be still and know that I am God."
Psalm 46:10

I was raised in a loving Christian home where I was taught about Christ and taken to church every time the doors were open. Though I was saved as a teenager — I became very rebellious when I went to college. At about age 25, a friend started taking me to church again. For a while, I had a close relationship with God, reading my Bible daily and being active in church. Then I chose to marry a non-Christian. I justified this decision by telling myself that my "good" ways would rub off on him. Unfortunately, quite the opposite happened. I found myself sleeping in on Sunday mornings and being unaffected by foul language or movies I once would have found offensive. Reading the Bible and praying became something I knew I should be doing, but just couldn't seem to find time for.

This is where my life was when I became pregnant with my first child. When I was about 15 weeks into my pregnancy, the doctor called and told us that some routine blood work had revealed that the baby probably had severe birth defects. I was devastated! At that instant all of the joy went out of my pregnancy and I became terrified of what the future held for us. I was inconsolable. I cried all night long. The next morning I decided to just throw myself into work and try to get my mind off of the "unknown." That day my commute was about 1 ½ hours long. I sobbed and prayed <u>out loud</u> the entire way there. The people around me in traffic no doubt thought I had lost my mind! I begged God to make everything okay. I knew I couldn't handle the situation. I was scared, angry, confused and I had never felt so alone.

I arrived at work with red swollen eyes and a runny nose, probably looking like a real sight! At that time, I was a mental health counselor at nursing homes around the Atlanta area. I decided I would see one of my patients who probably wouldn't notice my disheveled appearance. I had been seeing this patient two to four times a month for about one year. In that time, he had never known my name or spoken to me except to say, "Lady! Lady! Don't let them hurt me!"

That morning began like every other visit. I held his hand and tried to provide comfort and reassurance while he cried out. All of a sudden, he became very quiet. He sat straight up in bed (he had never done that before), turned toward me and said, "You're going to have a baby." I was stunned and speechless! I managed to say "yes". He looked at me very seriously and said in an earnest tone of voice, "Dawn, don't you know? God in heaven sent that baby to you." Then as suddenly as he had stopped, he lay down and began crying out. At that moment I had complete peace. I felt like God Himself had wrapped His arms around me and said, "It's okay. I am in control!" I knew that whatever happened with the baby, we would be alright. The doctors persistently tried to do more extensive tests, but I refused. At that point, it simply didn't matter. I would have the baby God had chosen for me.

God did bless us with a healthy child. I believe He let me go through that experience to not only remind me that **He** is in control, but also to bring me back to Him. That was about seven years ago. Since then, there have been times when I was distraught, overwhelmed, and afraid. I have struggled, at times, to see evidence of God in difficult situations. What I have learned is that even when I can't see God, can't feel His presence, He IS there. He is on His throne!! No matter what happens in my life, He IS there! Even in my times of doubt and unfaithfulness, He is ever faithful! Now when I am facing a challenging situation, my patient's face will come to mind, as if God is reminding me that there is no challenge He can't handle.

THE POWER OF THE WORD
by
JIMMY SCROGGINS

"So is My Word that goes out from my mouth: It will not return to me empty, but will accomplish what I desire and achieve the purpose for which I sent it, no matter who Satan tries to use or what Satan does to interfere. Nothing can stand against the Holy Spirit when He is at work bringing a lost one to faith in Jesus."
Adaptation from Isaiah 55:11

It was sometime in the late spring of 1997, I think in April. Our son, Jason, had not been saved very long. A friend of his, I will call him Larry, had a bit of a problem. It seemed that Larry had gone to Panama City for spring break with a pistol that had been stolen from our home a few months prior. Larry didn't steal it, but he wound up with it. As I understand it, Larry had been involved in some activities that he should not have been involved in, but he had decided to turn his life around and was trying to join the Navy. To do what he wanted to do in the Navy, he needed a certain level of security clearance.

He was in Panama City with two other guys and, as they were driving down the street, one of them got into an altercation with someone on the sidewalk. Long story short, one of the guys jumped out of the car with a knife and cut the fellow pretty bad, bad enough that he almost died. Larry and the other companion went on down the street in the car, but were stopped by the police. Larry had stuffed the pistol up under himself to hide it, but the police found it and Larry was charged with carrying a concealed weapon. It is my understanding that a concealed weapon is a misdemeanor in Florida unless it is stolen, then it becomes a felony. Larry couldn't get his clearance in the Navy with a felony on his record.

One night Jason told me about this and that Larry was going to call to see if I could help him. And sure enough he called, explained it all, and asked for my help. I agreed to help, as long as I didn't have to lie.

About two weeks later Larry called back and said, "Mr. Scroggins, I've got to come and see you about this," and he did and brought his mamma with him.

I told Jason I was going to try to lead him to faith in Jesus, so I put my Bible and a CWT witnessing tract on the table. Larry and his mother came in and sat down. He went over the whole deal with me and again asked for my help. I reminded him of our previous conversation and told him again that I would do anything I could to help except lie.

Then I said, "Now, we have gotten that all out of the way. It is a done deal. You don't have to worry about me anymore." He said that he was satisfied and really appreciated it. Then I said, "Now I want to ask you a question. Did it ever occur to you that God might have something in mind for you and you are messing up His plan?" To which he replied, "Yes sir, I have been thinking about that some lately." We went through a number of verses about God's purpose, our problem, God's provision, and how we should respond.

Just as we were getting down to the response part, Jason cranked his truck. Normally that wouldn't be a problem, but this wasn't normal. The exhaust system had gone bad and I was in the process of replacing it. Everything was done except connecting the mufflers, so when he cranked it, one wall away from us, there was an unexpected, earsplitting roar. Jason sat there revving it up over and over for what seemed like a long time.

(I used to race some over at Road Atlanta near Gainesville. On Sunday morning from eleven to twelve, because of complaints from the churches near there, we could not have any race engines running. Not being a Christian at the time, and even since, I have wondered if that was because there was more power evident at the race track than in the churches.)

Well, on this particular night the power was right there with Larry and Satan had nothing that would overcome the Holy Spirit! Larry never wavered, never lost focus, and I didn't slow down as I explained to him about repentance, trust, faith, and calling on the name of the Lord. Today Larry is a fine young business owner with a sweet wife and child. But most importantly, he is on his way to Heaven and the verse I started with holds true.

I did approach his mother also and she assured me that she was indeed a believer. I know that means a lot to Larry because she passed away a few years back and he has the sure hope of seeing her again.

SAVED AND SET FREE!
by
Jimmy Scroggins

"I have come that they may have life and have it more abundantly".
John 10:10

March 21, 1997 marked the beginning of a lesson in God's faithfulness and a true spiritual breakthrough in our lives. Our older son, Jason, had, for quite some time, been getting farther and farther away from us and from God. He was only 18, but I knew he was drinking and using marijuana at the least. I did not realize how far into drugs he had gotten.

About three weeks prior to that date, I was sitting on the front porch praying. Be careful what you pray for. I had no idea that God would respond the way He did. The gist of the prayer was this: "God, you have blessed us real good with Jason and Stephen and I thank you for it. It is a huge responsibility and we have tried to raise them in a way pleasing to You. You know the way Jason is headed, as well as I do and You know we have done as much about it as we can. I have come to understand that he belongs to You, not me, so I release him back to You. Please do whatever it takes to deliver him from this disaster he is headed toward."

In less than three weeks, Jason was sitting in Bartow County jail charged with selling LSD at school. I thought to myself, "Hey God, what's up with that?! Didn't I ask You to deliver him from that? If this is deliverance, spare me!" I decided Jason was either going to change his ways or sit in jail. Sitting in jail was NOT what God had in mind. When Jason called that night, I knew from the moment I started talking to him that something was different. It wasn't that he had changed his ways, it was that the Lord changed his heart. Dewey Davidson, our pastor at the time, had been to see Jason. He talked pretty straight to him and the Holy Spirit led him to faith in Jesus. He hasn't been the same since!

I wish I could say that was all there was to it and everyone lived happily from then on out, but this isn't a fairy tale. Jason was sentenced to eight years. He was required to spend six months in a diversion center and the balance on probation. The whole experience was like walking a tightrope. The attorney told me just how close Jason came to spending two or three **years** in a state prison. Thankfully, the District Attorney would not recommend prison for an 18 year old boy on his first offense, but one slip-up at the diversion center or on probation had the very real potential to put him there. (One of his friends, who was 17 and in a different situation, went to prison.) Selling drugs at school is treated more seriously and rightfully so.

Even though we got a lot of support and encouragement from friends during this time, it was the promise of Jesus to never leave us or forsake us that helped the most. Our God is 100 percent faithful and He demonstrated that to us. It has nothing to do with following a formula or anything else we could do. He cannot deny Himself. Even when we are unfaithful, He remains faithful and He has demonstrated that to us over and over. When things looked bad, I remembered that Jason belonged to God and even if he did go to prison, God would be there with him. I made a decision not to worry. It was God's problem because Jason was His.

In **John 10:10**, the second part, Jesus said, *"I have come that they may have life and have it more abundantly."* In nearly 25 years of being a believer, I have experienced that abundant life over and over. When Paul writes about the "peace that passes all understanding" I have a little bit, a tiny glimmer of an idea about what that means. When someone said they didn't understand how we could be so calm under the circumstances, we could point them to the Lord and say, it is all on Him!

I am grateful to be able to say that Jason met all of the requirements to be granted first offender status and have his record cleared. He has been faithfully serving our Lord ever since and active in mission work at his church.

Another example of God's blessing occurred in connection with Jason's salvation...

When I was 13 years old, my daddy whipped me for the last time and made me cry. I took 2 vows that day. First was that he would never do that again. That vow was never tested. As for the other vow, believing tears to be a sign of weakness, I vowed to never cry again for anyone or anything...and I didn't, for about 38 years.

After I surrendered to Jesus, around the age of 35, I prayed for release from the vow and even tried to produce tears by sheer strength of the will...nothing worked...until March 23, 1997. On that Sunday, Jason went to church and professed his faith in Jesus publicly. Finally, the Lord released me or maybe I just wasn't able to hold it back any longer. Now I can't stop.

The song that I remember that day summed up my feelings completely. It was the chorus that goes, "I will enter His gates with thanksgiving in my heart, I will enter His courts with praise, I will say this is the day that the Lord has made, I will rejoice for He has made me glad." On that day, in spite of the events of the previous few days and knowing there was a rocky road ahead, life was indeed abundant. Life is always abundant with Jesus and that abundant life produces the peace that passes understanding. The problem is that we are often so focused on our circumstances that we don't recognize it.

A HERITAGE OF FAITHFULNESS
by
ARLEEN SHOOK

*"But I lavish unfailing love for a **thousand generations** on those who love me and obey my commands"*
Exodus 20:6 (emphasis added)

Life is so interesting – it lets you become different things to different folks. In my lifetime, I've become a daughter, a granddaughter, a wife, a daughter-in-law, a sister-in-law, a mother, a mother-in-law and a grandmother (to list a few). I am so blessed to have had two grandmothers who loved the Lord, who loved me, prayed for me and lived an abundant life in front of me. I remember baking cakes and pies, working in the flowers and spending the night at my grandmother's house. It was a real treat just to be near them and enjoy their hugs, love and encouragement.

God gave me a beautiful, radiant, loving and godly mother. I learned everything at her knee. She taught me about Jesus and showed me daily how to live for Him. She and my daddy took me to church on Sundays, Wednesdays, to Gas, WMU and choir... and anything else anytime the church doors were opened.

I am an only child and she was a homemaker, so we spent many happy hours playing, sewing doll clothes, cooking and talking. We always had wonderful communication between us. She has always been my best friend. I am so blessed.

I also have a wonderful, godly father who has loved my mother and me with the most unselfish love ever known. He has taught me so much about how my heavenly father loves me. He and my mother were wonderful examples of the way Christians should live. They very lovingly led me to the Lord when I was ten years old. Today, my dad is my prayer warrior partner...and the best one ever!

When Roger and I were dating, Roger was of another faith. I became very burdened because Roger had never actually asked Jesus into his heart. On a date one night, God gave me the opportunity to lead him to Christ. What a privilege!

After our marriage, Roger and I enjoyed building our home together. One of the greatest thrills any woman can know is the birth of her children. Our home was wonderfully blessed with two of the greatest sons in the world. There is just no higher calling in the world than the calling to be "Mom". I enjoyed every minute of their childhood, most of their adolescence, and now their adulthood. Most of all, I am thankful that we saw both our sons accept Christ as Savior and be baptized. God has indeed blessed us!

I am so very thankful for my two daughters-in-law. They are such a blessing in my life. I jokingly tell them that I love them because I didn't have to potty train them or go with them through adolescence. Truthfully, they are beautiful to me because they love my sons. Again, God has blessed!

Looking back, things have been good – but, when I became a grandmother, everything just got "gooder". Being a grandmother is the best experience you could ever imagine! When our oldest grandson, Blake, was about to become two years old, we were driving down the road one day and saw two John Deere tractors. Knowing that tractors are Blake's favorite thing in the world, I said "Look Blake! There are TWO tractors. Like you are going to be TWO, there are TWO tractors." From that day on, you could ask, "Blake, how old are you going to be?" His reply was always – "I'll be two tractors!"

On his birthday, I called to wish him a happy birthday and to sing to him. After belting out the Birthday song, I said to him, "Blake, Honey loves you THIS much!" There was a pause on the other end of the phone line. Then he said, "Honey, I love you two tractors!" WOW! I bet there have been very few women in the whole world who have ever been loved "two tractors"! I am blessed indeed!!!!

I am so thankful for the heritage of Christian love and family love that God has so abundantly given to me. I'm thankful most of all for Jesus Christ who willingly, lovingly and voluntarily laid down His life on the cross, stretched out His arms and said, "Arleen, I love you THIS much!" He didn't love me with a tractor…He loved me with a cross. Hallelujah! What a Savior!

At this point in my life, my concern is finishing well. I pray daily that God would protect my witness and ministry and our home and family. I continually ask the Father to help me be an encourager to others, especially the children here at Tabernacle. They have no idea how much I love them and desire for them to see Jesus' love in me.

There is great joy in helping others along the way. It is so important not to hurry through life, but to stop and invest time in children and others along the way. I pray that like those beautiful and godly women in my heritage that God would find me faithful to His Word and His calling. I pray that I will be able to tell my grandchildren, Blake, Chandler, Haley, Maggie, and Rylee about the love of Christ and how much He loves them. I pray that they will see Jesus in me and they will be drawn to His unfailing love. The words to the song, Find us Faithful, written by John Mohr, have meant so much to me:

*We're pilgrims on the journey of the narrow road,
And those who've gone before us line the way.
Cheering on the faithful, encouraging the weary,
Their lives a stirring testament to God's sustaining grace.
Surrounded by so great a cloud of witnesses,
Let us run the race not only for the prize,
But as those who've gone before us,
Let us leave to t hose behind us the heritage
Of faithfulness passed on through Godly lives.
After all our hopes and dreams have come and gone,
And our children sift through all we've left behind,
May the clues that they discover and the memories they uncover,
Become the light that leads them to the road we each must find.
Oh, may all who come behind us find us faithful.
May the fire of our devotion light the way,
May the footprints that we leave, lead them to believe,
And the lives we live inspire them to obey.
Oh, may all who come behind us find us faithful.*

MY HERO, MY SISTER
by
CINDY SMITH

"Therefore, if anyone is in Christ, he is a new creation; the old has gone, the new has come!"
II Corinthians 5:17

She was born five years after me...I remember jumping up and down on my grandmothers front porch as my dad called to tell me that my brother and I had a sister!

From the beginning I loved being the big sister. Caring for her was a joy to me.

Life went along fine until I hit about 13. Family dynamics changed and I moved away from my family. My sister and I grew apart.

(My sister is one of the most caring individuals I know! Once there was a cat in the road that had been hit by a car. In her rearview mirror she looked in time to see the injured cat raise it's head. She stopped the car, ran back to the cat, picked it up, and carried it to a vet where it was treated. The cat "Cosmo" went on to live a healthy cat life!)

Our Christian parents loved all five of us kids the same, but we all took different approaches to life. Life did seem unfair to all of us at some point... maybe it seemed the most unfair to my sister. After experiencing sexual abuse from a relative and a rape by a neighbor (also a member of her church)...things went from bad to worse. To deal with her pain, my sister shut off her emotions along with any contact with God. After she had been treated so badly by religious people ...she cut off anyone that might have been able to help her. I honestly understand where she was coming from.

After many years of drug abuse and many other abusive choices, my prayers, my parents' prayers and the prayers of many others were visibly answered. After 26 years of shutting off the One who could help her deal with her pain, she became broken. There was no where to go but to her Creator. She checked herself into a rehab center where she experienced detoxing of her body and her soul. For the first time in several decades she was able to feel emotions. God healed her.

When my sister checked into rehab she was suicidal. I was so heartbroken for her and to be honest, for me. I ministered to hurting women all week long, yet I could not reach my own sister. I prayed for the counselors and others that would be helping her.

After nine months of treatment my sister asked to move to Georgia to be near me! WOW! I could not believe it...I was full of mixed emotions...but the feeling that stood out the most was excitement! God was bringing her to me and my family!

After being clean for over six years, my sister now ministers alongside me to girls, women and families through the Bartow County Women's Resource Center. She is now a new creation (**II Corinthians 5:17**) and is able to reach those who walk in her old shoes. She is constantly giving her testimony of sanctification and transformation to all who will listen.

I wrote this as a testimony to God's faithfulness to my sister, her daughter and all of our family...and as a big thank you to my sister for her huge loving impact on Cartersville, Georgia! Thank you Joan!

OUR STORIES OF FAITH
by
JUDY SMITH (with J. B.)

"All things work together for the good of those who love the Lord and are called according to His purpose."
Romans 8:28

It would take an ocean of ink to write all the ways our dear Lord and Savior, Jesus Christ who has blessed us in our wonderful 44 years of marriage.

He blessed us first of all, by choosing us before the foundation of the world. **John 15-16** (KJV). He blessed me with a great Godly husband in J. B., as well as two wonderful sons, Rhett and Rodney, and our precious daughter, Regina. Rodney and Lisa have three amazing boys and Regina and Joel added three equally amazing daughters and a son into our family. What a gift they are to all of us.

I was blessed with a wonderful mother and daddy, six brothers and four sisters. I was number ten in the line-up. My mother was not able to attend church, but lived out her faith in Jesus Christ each day at home. She prayed without ceasing. She selflessly chose to care for my oldest sister whose brain was damaged at an early age from fever. She would not put her in a home as the doctor suggested, but took care of her until she was physically unable. Our family was very poor, but we were blessed with an abundance of love.

My daddy would take us to church sometimes and drop us off. Other times we had to walk to get there. Daddy was a very loving, compassionate man. He lived in an orphanage until he was five years old. My mother and daddy were deeply in love and were married 60 years before his death in 1980. She lived until 1998, and there was not a day that passed in which she did not miss him. She said the secret to their long marriage was **Ephesians 4:26-27** (KJV). *"Be ye angry, and sin not. Let not the sun go down upon your wrath, neither give peace to the devil."* Mother said when Daddy died in her arms, he went very peacefully. I have never known for sure if he was saved, but I have prayed that he was.

J. B. was raised on a farm in Gadsden, Alabama. His mother was a nurse and did her best to take care of the three children, but his daddy was an alcoholic who was very abusive. His mother didn't drive, so they didn't attend church. At nine years old he was saved. Praise the Lord! How great was the hand of our Father to protect and provide for J. B. in order to make him the man he is today. God was present to watch over him, his brother Bobby, and sister, Dorothy.

When I was almost seven years old, I was in a movie. The scene was a church with beautiful, stained glass window. The song playing was "Holy, Holy, Holy." My heart was so touched right then, I knew I wanted to know more about the "Holy One." I started helping in Bible School at a Methodist Church. Almost every Sunday we walked on a dirt road. In Bible School I helped serve Kook-aid with the songs and games.

The song I loved so much was "Into my heart, into my heart, come into my heart, Lord Jesus. Come in today, come into stay, come into my heart, Lord Jesus." I know He did. Praise the Lord! At 13 years old, during a revival, my brother, 16, and I went forward to join the church. I didn't have the counseling I needed, and drifted away after a few years. When J. B. and I married, he said we were always going to be in the Church.

In 1964 we joined Fair Oaks Baptist Church in Marietta. That year we were both baptized, and started faithfully attending the church. We were members until 1970. At that time, we went to Welcome All Baptist Church in Smyrna, where our kids all grew up. Many memories were made, and we all grew in our Christian walks more than ever. In 1988 we joined Orange Hill Baptist in Austell. In 2000 we moved to Acworth, and started to Tabernacle Baptist. We knew right away this was where God wanted us. We praise the Lord for our wonderful pastor, Sunday school classes, staff, choir, and a new family we love so much.

My first Scripture to learn was **Ephesians 4:32** (KJV). *"Be ye kind, one to another, tender hearted, forgiving one another."* I can't stay mad at anyone very long as this verse is embedded in my soul.

We had some real struggles with our son in his teenage years and for many years to follow. During our biggest trial, God assured us of His wonderful promise in **Romans 8:28** (KJV). *"All things work together for the good of those who love the Lord and are called according to His purpose."* We both claimed the verse, and clung to it. We had to really believe and take God at His Word. That verse is still one of our favorites.

When our first grandson was born with cerebral palsy and Celia dyskonesia syndrome, he had many special needs and health issues. One time he was going for a test to see if he had cystic fibrosis. I was praying so hard, but not letting God handle the situation. At 3 a.m. before the test, I was awakened and it was like "peace, peace, peace" flashed all over the room. Then a favorite Scripture came to my mind, **John 14:27** (KJV). *"Peace, I leave with you. Peace I give unto you; not as the world giveth, give I unto you. Let now your heart be troubled, neither let it be afraid."* That morning at 7a.m. I called our son, Rodney, and told him the test would be negative, and it was! Praise the Lord!

In 1997 our first granddaughter, Ashlyn, was very sick in the hospital, and she said she wanted to die. Of course, I was praying with all my heart. I opened the Lord's Book to **Psalms 4:3-5**, *"Oh my soul, why be so gloomy, and discouraged. Trust in God; I shall again praise Him for His wondrous help. He will make me smile again."* Wow, what an awesome God we serve!!

"To God be the glory, great things He hath done!" At every stage of our lives, it has been the presence of God, and the knowledge of His Word that has gotten us through. He has made the joy more joyful and the pain less painful. He is always faithful. May we be so faithful to Him.

THE MIRACLE OF ETERNAL LIFE
by
ROD STRICKLAND

"Jesus answered, 'I tell you the truth, no one can enter the kingdom of God unless he is born of water and the Spirit. Flesh gives birth to flesh, but the Spirit gives birth to spirit'"
John 3:5-6

The miracle of physical life occurred for me on January 20, 1943. My family was living in Brunswick, Georgia where my Dad was working at the ship yard, building Liberty ships during WWII. Mom had my baby sister after the war in a doctor's office in Screven, Georgia. She almost died during the delivery. Thank God, He spared her life. My sister's birth brought the total number of children to five.

After the war Dad became an auto body and paint repairman and opened his own shop in Jesup, Georgia. I can remember going to the shop when I was very small and enjoying seeing my dad turn wrecks into beautiful automobiles again. I can remember being proud of my dad because of his unusual talent for repair and painting cars. Other repairmen would visit his shop to get pointers from my dad.

Little did I know at this time there was great turbulence in our family. I learned later in life that my dad had begun to drink heavily and was abusive to my mother (physically & emotionally). He was not only drinking but also running around with other women. One late afternoon in 1951 I remember my dad coming out of the bedroom with a suitcase. My mom was crying. I asked Dad where he was going and he said he was going on a business trip. That was the last time I saw my dad for a long time.

We were living in a modest middle class home at the time and we had to move right after my dad left. We moved out of town to the edge of the country in a little house with no running water or electricity. I remember being frightened as there were no locks on the doors or screens in the windows. I also remember that my mother was not afraid in the least and that gave me some assurance. Mom still had four children at home to take care of and to feed. Marvin and Marion (twins) were 12; I was 8; and my baby sister, Faye, was 5. Mom had no job and there was no food or money. I don't remember how we made it, but I do remember eating a lot of pancakes and syrup. I never heard my mother complain or cry in anguish. She was a strong Christian and we never missed going to church. We had no car so we would catch a ride with someone. I remember that my mother prayed a lot.

My uncle, Tip, came home from being overseas in the merchant marines and started to live with us. Things got better. Uncle Tip provided food and other essentials. We moved back to town to government housing. It was better, but downgrading to have to live in this type of environment. I was always embarrassed when my friends found out where I lived. This began a long journey of sad, sullen, feelings of worthlessness. I became rebellious and hard to get along with. I was always ready to fight at the least provocation. In short, I was miserable, lonely and bitter. My mother was always one to encourage and strived to lead us to a desire to give our lives to the Lord. I didn't take too well to that notion.

I joined the Air Force as soon as I was 18, hoping I would find a new life with some new reasons to live. Little did I know that this decision would change my life forever toward a new direction with great expectations. I did well in the Air Force and soon realized that if I applied myself I could achieve more than I ever thought I could. I earned the title of honor student in the tech school and was awarded the honor of choosing my overseas assignment. I could have chosen any base, but I chose Japan. I didn't know at the time but God was arranging a meeting with me in Japan that would change my life forever.

Japan was still recovering from the perils of WWII and the exchange rate for American currency was 360 yen to the dollar. We all thought we were rich as we exchanged our money to yen and were enjoying all that went with having a lot of money to spend. I began to party and concentrated on having a good time. I sank deeper and deeper into a sinful, godless life. I met another man from my home town on the main base and we became friends. I quickly found out that this new friend was a Christian and he would constantly invite me to go to church with him. I wasn't interested, but I finally did agree to go to a meeting with him in downtown Misawa at the Christian Service Men's center. That night I came to a crossroad in my life.

The preacher was a missionary from New Zealand to the Japanese people. He was a fire and brimstone type of preacher and didn't beat around the bush about what life was all about. The preaching began to convict me that I needed to get my life right with God. I went forward during the invitation and asked God to save me. My friend who invited me knelt with me at the altar and another friend that I worked with knelt on the other side. The preacher helped me say the sinner's prayer. When I got up off my knees I suddenly realized that something special had happened to me. I felt revived, clean, excited and new. I later found out that I had been "born again" through the Holy Spirit of God. That was April 3, 1962. I was baptized by Brother Midgley on April 7th in a local Japanese Baptist church. I can truly say that I have never been the same since.

The first person who I wanted to know about my conversion was my mother. I wrote her a long letter telling her about my new found faith. Of course, she was delighted as this had been her prayer for me for years. We enjoyed a great time of fellowship together until her home going on January 7, 1991.

I found a wonderful group of Christian friends in Japan and grew a lot in the next year and a half while I was still stationed there. I am still in touch with several of those friends to this day, including Maxi Howard, the friend that invited me to church that night.

The Lord blessed me with a wonderful wife in 1970 and Dianna and I have been together for 37 years. He also gave me two wonderful daughters, Sonia Hattaway, my oldest daughter, and Shanda Strickland, my youngest. Sonia is a pastor's wife and also teaches school. She loves God and is a great witness for the Lord. Shanda is soon to be married to a good Christian man. Shanda got a degree in Missions from Liberty University and served her Lord in China with the Southern Baptist Missions board. Shanda is also a great witness and loves the Lord. I also am blessed with three precious grandchildren.

I'm sixty-four years old now and I often think back to my childhood and the rough times I went through. I always thank my God for my Christian mother who always had a positive outlook on life and constantly encouraged me to give myself to the Lord. Thank you, Mom, for your prayers.

Thank you, blessed Lord, for Your mercy, Who answered my Mom's prayers and gave me the wonderful "MIRACLE OF ETERNAL LIFE."

OUR STORIES OF FAITH
by
RIC AND ANDREA SUNDSTROM

"Now all glory to God, who is able, through his mighty power at work within us, to accomplish infinitely more than we might ask or think."
Ephesians 3:20 (NLT)

When I (Andrea) was a teenager and then in my early 20s, I made all my own choices about how I would live, what I would wear and where I would go. I really had no conscience as to any right or wrong. I thought love depended on my outward appearance. No matter what I did, the need was never met.

Then, in 1977, while living in Knoxville, Tennessee a man knocked on my door. He was crying as he invited me to revival at the church down the street. He said that he couldn't understand why people would line up to play bingo, but no one wanted to come to the house of God and hear about Jesus, Whom he loved. I was curious about this love that would make him knock on my door to seek me with tears. I was afraid to go to his church by myself, so I wasn't going to go, but my neighbor said she would go with me. If it had not been for her, I probably would not have gone.

I went to the revival and there I heard the life-changing message that Jesus Christ loved me and died to pay the penalty for my sin. I accepted Him and had a life changing experience with the One Who truly loves me. Now, instead of relying on myself, I turn to Him to teach me and to help me choose right and turn away from wrong. So now, I am truly loved and can love others in return.

When I (Ric) was 12 years old, I accepted Jesus into my heart, but I did not change my self-will. I spent many years living for pleasure and for myself. Four of those years were spent in the Navy, while I continued on the same destructive path.

By the time I was 34, I was deep into alcoholism. I lost everything I had. I eventually had to go to court for a DUI. The District Attorney looked at me and said,

"I'll tell you what. If you won't help yourself, I can't help you either. You need to go to AA." This was not what I wanted to hear, but I knew I was at the bottom and had no where to go.

Tabernacle **Stories of Faith**

I went to First Step Recovery and they mistook me for the keynote speaker! They soon realized I was there for help. It was a very humbling process, but it was through AA and the steps that they taught me that I realized I was powerless over alcohol and that I needed to trust in God to deliver me. On October 6, 1992 I made a decision to return to the Jesus I had accepted as a 12 year old boy and to do things His way. He gave me victory over alcohol and He gave me my life back…only BETTER!

Five years later, I met Andrea. We fell in love and got married. We began to search out churches and Tabernacle was it! We fell in love with Pastor Dewey Davidson and we loved the music. Pastor Dewey came to our house and blessed it (we were renting at the time). A week later, the owners came and asked us if we wanted to buy the home. We said, "Yes!"

About a week after we joined Tabernacle, Andrea came to me and talked to me about tithing. I had never done that before, but decided it was what God wanted. We began to tithe to God. Two weeks later, I started my own business as a carpenter and God has blessed our business ever since. Turning my life and will over to Jesus was the best decision I've ever made. He changed my life, changed it beyond all my expectations or my wildest dreams. (**Ephesians 3:20**)

CALLING ON THE LORD
by
JEAN W. TATUM

"The Lord is near to all who call on him, to all who call on him in truth."
Psalm 145:18

When I received Kim Lewis' letter asking for testimonies of answered prayers, times of crisis, family blessings, etc., I had walked to the mailbox. On the way back to the house, I opened the letter and began to read and at the same time I began to cry. My thoughts returned to October 31, 2003 and the events of that day. I have tried not to put the accounts of this event on paper, but cannot get away from the feeling that I must.

My granddaughter, Nichole, who resides in Florida, had her birthday on October 31, 2003. Around 2:30 or 3:30 in the afternoon I had called her to wish her happy birthday. Little did I know that would be one of the hardest times of my life. As you know, this is the day everyone celebrates Halloween. My husband and I were at home in the evening as children came to the house to get treats. Other members of our family were at Tabernacle having fun. Our telephone rang and on the end of the line was Mike Ronsisvalle, who is the husband of Chrystal, who is a sister to Nichole. He asked how we were, but then said he had some bad news and that Connor was gone. Connor is Nichole's son. At first I thought someone had kidnapped him. I asked where and how. He said "no" Connor was dead. He drowned that afternoon in the family pool. I cannot clearly remember what happened after that other than I knew all the family had gathered at the house and I needed to be on my way to Florida as soon as possible. It so happened Urby, my husband, and I had planned to go to the mountains the next day and our bags were packed so only some changes in clothing for a warm climate were necessary.

Around 10:30 p.m. we were in the car and on our way – my husband, Urby, my daughter, Vicki, and her husband, John, and my sister, Geraldine. As we sat in the car at Geraldine's house, Vicki prayed for us and all our family as we made this sad journey. Hardly a word was spoken on that eight to nine hour drive. I was silently praying for strength to face my family there in Florida.

A peace came over me that I have not been able to explain nor have I tried, but as surely as I write these accounts today, God sent an angel to ride and guide our journey that night. The words of a song came to my mind, "surely the presence of the Lord is in this place," fit because His presence was in the car that night. As we were on the beeline causeway that led from Orlando to their home due east to Cocoa and Viera Beach, the sun began to rise and I began to pray for strength to face my granddaughter. God was with me in such a wonderful way as I saw her spring from the house into my arms as if she had been waiting for us to get there. God was there with us during those sad days and has been with us these years since that sad event. I do not know why this tragic event had to take place, nor do I question God. All I know is if you know Him and will call upon His Name in your times of need, He will hear you and answer. I also know that you do not need to wait for a crisis to pray, but to pray daily and He will walk with you each and every day of your life. I pray that by writing about a part of this tragic event in my family's life, God will reveal to those who read not to forget to pray and will thank God for all their blessings. And if by chance there is someone who does not know Him, they will humble themselves and pray and receive Him. If so, they can have the same peace I felt in a time of crisis.

TOTAL SURRENDER
By
MAX TATUM

"Therefore we do not lose heart. Though outwardly we are wasting away, yet inwardly we are being renewed day by day."
II Corinthians 4:16

I felt the call of God on my life at an early age, 12 or 13. I sensed His presence being with me very strongly at certain times, on the farm where I was born and raised.

But, I got involved in other things like sports. Later, after Janet and I got married, I got deeply involved in the party life, basically the "fast lane" of life.

One day, while playing golf, I could again sense the presence of God calling me. At this time, I was in the insurance business and thinking I had "arrived" being in my mid-thirties. This went on for some time.

I was getting burned out in insurance, so I changed to another profession of sales, a tangible product of maintenance supplies.

I went on the road with U.S. Industrial and soon found out I needed someone other than myself. I was tired of the way I was living. I was 40 years old and my life was miserable.

We started going to the church where my son was attending at the time. It was a growing church and a lot of people were going. That intrigued me and moved me to see what was really going on there. I needed help and those Christian friends at church knew that. They knew that I needed Jesus.

Being raised in a Christian home and in a primitive Baptist Church, Pine Grove Baptist Church, I knew what I had to do to be saved. I do not remember the day or month for certain, I think it was October. I remember the place and the year. It was 1976. I pulled off onto the side of the road near Neel's Gap Mountain close to Blairsville, GA. There, I gave it all to Him and received Jesus as my personal Savior. Those mountains seemed to come to life with a brilliance I had never seen before. I was FREE! I was a new person and this newness I found is renewed every day of my life (**II Corinthians 4:16**) to life eternal.

I gave up nothing to receive all. I am now, as of this writing, 71 years old and I would not go back for the world.

GOD IS MY PEACE
by
SANDY TAYLOR

"Do not be anxious about anything, but in everything, by prayer and petition, with thanksgiving, present your requests to God. And the peace of God, which transcends all understanding, will guard your heart and your minds in Christ Jesus."
Philippians 4:6-7

The year 2004 was the year that my life totally changed and would never be the same again. It was not as I had expected. My youngest child, Leah Taylor, graduated from high school that year and I thought I would be experiencing empty nest syndrome as she left in the fall to go to UGA. However, in November, before I had time to adjust to that, my 34 year old son, Russ Cowart, was diagnosed with stage 4 stomach cancer. We began trying to find out where Russ could get the best treatment. His sister,

Risa Womack, searched to try to find the best cancer hospitals for him to go to. We went to several doctors and then to M. D. Anderson in Houston, Texas, but got the same prognosis at each place. We were praying for a miracle – for Russ to be healed.

I felt so helpless and knew there was nothing I could do to fix this situation and that we had to depend on God to help us get through. Many people were praying for Russ and our family. I just could not believe the coincidence that Russ lost his dad when he was 8 years old and his sister, Risa, was 6, and now his daughter Kristen was 8 and his son Zach was 5, and they were facing the loss of their dad. I tried not to ask why, because I don't question why when good things happen in my life that I don't deserve. Many days I didn't feel like I could even function, but somehow with God's help I was able to take him to doctors' appointments and do most of what I needed to do. If I wasn't available, friends or family were always there to help.

Our lives seemed to go up and down like a roller coaster. We would get a little bit of hope and then have it snatched away. We spent much time in doctors' offices and hospitals. Each time Russ was given a low percentage of survival, he was so optimistic. Once he was told that his survival rate was less than 10% and he said that if five out of a 100 made it he might be one of the five. I believed with all my heart that God would heal him and what a testimony he would have. Looking back, I don't think I was accepting reality, but I don't think I could have gotten through the last days of Russ' life without the hope for a cure. Russ did manage to outlive his prognosis of six months to a year. As each month went by, Russ would say that maybe the next month a cure would be found that would heal him. It was hard for me to think that in this short time I might not have my son in my life. What I affirm now is that God did answer our prayers and heal Russ, it just wasn't the way I wanted.

The good attitude Russ had throughout his last 13 months helped all of us so much. He always had a positive attitude. When we were down many times he would be the one to encourage us. He would tell me not to treat him like he was sick. I did try, but it was very hard. All of the doctors and nurses who helped take care of Russ were wonderful. It seemed like at the lowest point in our lives we not only had many friends and family to help us get through, but also many new folks became friends. Russ was such an inspiration, not only to me, but to other cancer patients with his wonderful outlook. When he would go to the Hope Center for chemo, he and a couple of other patients along with the nurses would be joking and actually enjoying their time there. One lady even said that taking chemo was something she looked forward to, kind of a highlight in her week.

Once when Russ was in the hospital and in very much pain I prayed for God to let me swap places with him and for the cancer to be in my body. But that wasn't God's plan. I said to Steve, my husband, "If only I could swap places with him. Any mother would do that." And he said, "Any daddy would to." I realized then that even though Russ was not his biological son he loved him just as much as I did. I knew that having Steve in my life was a wonderful blessing from God. As I looked at my son, suffering so much, I thought about Jesus and all the pain he endured for my sins. I looked up and asked God how He could have allowed His Son to die for me? I knew that it was more than I could comprehend.

Everyone was so good to us during Russ' illness and we received many cards. It seemed that **Philippians 4:6-7** just kept appearing in cards, in our Sunday School lesson or the preacher's sermon. One day, my daughter, Leah, who was a sophomore at UGA, sent me an email that said, "Mom, read **Philippians 4:6-7**; it's good!!" I called and told her that Scripture just kept coming up and she said it did with her too. Beginning with verse 6 Paul says, *"Don't worry about anything; instead pray about everything. Tell God what you need, and thank him for all he has done. Then you will experience God's peace, which exceeds anything we can understand. His peace will guard your hearts and minds as you live in Christ Jesus." (New Living Translation)* I knew it was not a coincidence that this Scripture kept coming up. I believe God knew these were the verses I needed at the time, but being slow to figure that out myself, He had to keep sending them to me through different people.

Russ went into the hospital the week before Christmas 2005. We had been excited because the way his chemo was scheduled he would not be taking chemo during Christmas, so we thought he would feel better and maybe enjoy the holiday time with his children and family. We soon realized he would probably not be coming home from the hospital at all. His aunt brought a small tree and put in his room. He was getting weaker each day. The day after Christmas he told Steve he was so glad he made it through Christmas because he didn't want his children to have the memory of his death on Christmas. After much pain and suffering, Russ passed away on December 30, 2005. I was holding his hand as he took his last breath. After a short time there was a beautiful smile on his face. I believe that was a gift to me from God, a sign that Russ was with Him at the moment the smile appeared. Russ always assured us that he was "absolutely positively certain" of his salvation and that he was not afraid of dying because he knew he would be with Jesus. He looked forward to seeing Jesus face to face, but knew that we would be sad to see him go.

I thank God that He has given us the peace that exceeds our understanding to get through these times of sorrow and grief. Even when my heart was so broken and sad, I had peace. Hindsight is such a wonderful thing. I can see God's hand in many circumstances in my life. I know that He brought certain people into my life to help me, to pray for me, and to be there during this time in my life. There is a hole in my heart that cannot be mended, and I miss Russ each and every day. But I am so thankful God allowed me the privilege of being his mom for 36 years and that He gave me a loving family and friends to help during this difficult time. I know that even though Russ is not with me physically, he will always be a part of our family and always be in my heart.

A few months after Russ' death, I was feeling very low and was having doubts about his salvation. I was just reading random Scriptures and flipping through my Bible when I looked down at the page and these words just seemed to leap off the page: *"Thy son liveth"* **John 4:53** *(KJV)*. These words spoken by Jesus, written in red, were written for me. I knew that God was speaking to me and assuring me that I would be with my son again one day in heaven.

Even during the dark days of Russ' illness and death and even when I was so sad, I felt God's presence and I could feel that prayers were being lifted up for my family and me. People have said to me, "You are so strong. I don't know how you do it." It has only been through the grace of God, that I had the strength to endure. I know that life goes on and Russ would not want me to be sad but to try to live life to the fullest. And so as I continue to live my life, I try to do so being thankful, thankful for the joy that Russ brought to me, for the lessons that he helped to teach, and for the impact that his life has had on others. I am also thankful for the gifts of family and friends who really bear with one another through pain and suffering. I may still have down days, but I live with the hope and promises from God that He is with me always and will carry me through the days of grief when I need Him the most.

MOVED, BUT NOT SHAKEN
(The story of the Tipper family:
Jonathan, Rhonda & Reagan)
by
JONATHAN TIPPER

"I sought the LORD, and he answered me; he delivered me from all my fears."
Psalm 34:4

Serving God in full-time ministry is a very humbling opportunity. Many times we think we're settled into a 'groove', when God decides that it is time for our faith and our character to be tested. Sometimes the testing comes in a light spring shower, but other times the testing comes in a storm unlike any you've ever experienced. This is our story; a story of faith and uncertainty, ultimately ending in the provision of the loving, sovereign God whom we serve.

In 2003, we were expecting the birth of our daughter, Reagan. We were in the midst of some important decision concerning Rhonda's work after the baby. After much deliberation and prayer, we decided that we would try to make it work with Rhonda staying at home with Reagan. This would mean that my job would be the only source of income. Less than a week after we made this decision, we found out that the budget situation in our church, where I was serving on staff, might leave me without a ministry position. We entered into some of the most unsettling weeks of our lives. Our security had been stripped from us. How would we be able to take care of our financial responsibilities with no jobs and care for a new baby? We began to pray for wisdom and guidance, trusting that God's plan was bigger, and better, than our circumstances.

I had the opportunity to spend a week in New Orleans in January of 2004, just weeks before Reagan was to be born. During that time, I began to feel an impression on my heart that moving to the main campus might be where God was leading us. Since I was already in my degree program through the seminary, it would not be a difficult move school-wise. However, the move would be another step of faith for me, Rhonda, and little Reagan. We spent time praying and weighed the option of going to seminary or waiting out things at church to see if my job would be safe. In March, we headed down to the seminary to visit as a family.

It turned out to be a great trip for us, and really helped us decide that we were supposed to be there. The move would enable me to finish my undergraduate studies more quickly and move into the Master's program. In July 2004, we packed up our belongings and moved from a 2300 square foot house that we dearly loved into a 650 square foot apartment. We thought it all to be quite the sacrifice, but God was preparing us for some of the most wonderful times and sweetest memories of our lives as a family.

We discovered the seminary campus in New Orleans to be a place where we were not just students ... we were new members of a wonderful family. Not long after we arrived, we began to meet other young couples with small children. God was bringing us all together as a support system at seminary. While we lacked material resources, our hearts were full with the joy of preparing together for the ministry God had called us to. Some of our dearest friends are from our experience in seminary, and we would not trade anything for the time we spent on the campus.

In May 2005, I graduated with a Bachelor of Arts degree in Christian Ministry and immediately began working toward a Master of Arts in Christian Education (MACE). We were preparing for another year at seminary. By this time, Rhonda had been hired as a teacher at Crescent City Christian School, and I had traded my U-Haul uniform in for a youth ministry position at Williams Boulevard Baptist Church in Kenner, Louisiana. Things were beginning to settle in for our family and we were excited to be serving in a wonderful church with so many wonderful people.

It was a significant time for us as some wounds from ministry were being healed. We were as content as we had ever been serving God together.

On Friday night, August 26th, we were enjoying a guys/girls night out. Some of the husbands were playing basketball in the seminary gym while our wives spent time together visiting and enjoying fellowship together. We had all been watching Hurricane Katrina make her way up through the Caribbean, and most recent reports were that she was going to make an eastward turn toward Mobile, Alabama. Hurricanes were always interesting times in New Orleans, because everyone had to watch and make sure that they were ready in case an evacuation order was made. We had already evacuated a year earlier for Hurricane Ivan, to find that only one-half inch of rain was the result. Katrina looked to be no different. We all went home that night confident that we were all going to be just fine.

Early Saturday morning (around 7am Central time), my dad called to ask if we were packing. I replied, "No, why?". Dad told us to turn on the television and look. During the night, Katrina had made a significant turn and was projected to make landfall in New Orleans as a Category 5 Hurricane. Since New Orleans is below sea level, this news meant that the entire city could be destroyed by Katrina's strong winds and intense storms. I woke Rhonda and we began to make plans to leave campus as soon as possible.

After we made a run to the gas station to get in line first, we packed the essentials. We only had 3 or 4 changes of clothes each, because we heard from the seminary administration that classes would resume the following Thursday, and that we could just consider this a mini-vacation. Around 11:45am, we locked the door to our apartment, said goodbye to some of our friends, and hit the road heading to Cartersville. Little did we know . . .

We arrived in Cartersville late Saturday night after a long day of driving. After church at Tabernacle and lunch with Rhonda's family, we went home to their house and watched the coverage of the hurricane all afternoon. By Sunday night, all signs were pointing to a quick 'vacation' and return home on Wednesday. It seemed as though New Orleans had dodged a bullet, and we were grateful, while at the same time saddened to see the devastation of Katrina to the Mississippi Gulf Coast.

Monday morning, August 29th, was going to be just another day. We turned on the television for an update to discover the horrific news that two of the levees in New Orleans had breached, and the city was being flooded at a rapid pace. This began a process of watching and waiting to see what damage the campus might suffer as a result of the widespread flooding. The next few weeks were some of the most difficult of our lives. A city that was rich in history and tradition would be mostly underwater, with reports of flooding over 80% of the entire city. We, along with every other seminary family, waited on news of the seminary and word of when we might return to check on our belongings. About the time that Katrina hit, Casting Crowns released their CD entitled *Lifesong*.

We found one of the songs from this album to be a great comfort during the time of waiting and uncertainty. The chorus from *"Praise You in This Storm"* says:

> *And I'll praise You in this storm / And I will lift my Hands*
> *'Cause You are who You are / No matter where I am*
> *And every tear I've cried / You hold in Your hand*
> *You've never left my side / And though my heart is torn*
> *I will praise You in this storm*

"This storm" was so much more than a hurricane. It was uncertainty and strife, not knowing if we had anything left, jobs to return to, or a place to go home to. We were in the middle of the deepest time of testing we had ever known, yet God used this song to provide peace and assurance that regardless of the size or intensity of the storm, He's still God. Wow!

After a long wait, we received word that we would be allowed to go back on campus for **one day** to assess our belongings and salvage anything we could. By this time we had heard that the back of campus, where we lived, had been under a great deal of floodwater. We had no idea what to expect. We rented a large moving truck and took a team of folks with us: Gary and Sherry Glaze, Steve and Tonia McCombs, Daniel Barnes, and Greg Davidson. My parents met us down in New Orleans, as they had been helping my sister sort through her dorm room on the seminary campus. We had no idea what to expect when we arrived on campus.

Driving into New Orleans was surreal. A city once alive with its rich history of arts and music seemed like an apocalyptic wasteland. On the east end of the city, there were no lights and no signs of life. As we pulled onto the seminary campus, we saw professor's houses that had been flooded, destroying everything they owned. Their belongings were piled high on the sidewalk, now just a pile of rubble. We got to our apartment and looked around. All over the place, we saw families huddled, sobbing as they had discovered their life's belongings destroyed. Wedding albums, heirlooms, treasured belongings that were now merely memories.

Rhonda and I walked the back steps together to our apartment, prepared for anything . . . expecting nothing. We were so overwhelmed to discover that our belongings were, for the most part, salvageable. How blessed we are!

So, here we are, over two years removed from Katrina. I never thought I would
experience anything like it, and I haven't experienced anything like it since. God has provided so much for us. Rhonda has a job teaching, while I am serving at Tabernacle Baptist Church. We have been blessed so much. A part of our hearts is still in New Orleans, because God taught us so much about trusting Him while we were there. Would we go back to seminary and do it all over again? Probably. You see, it's not about us . . . it's all about Him! We've

discovered that the call to serve God is an adventure, even a risk. I will always believe that Katrina was part of the risk. But looking back on our experience, I wouldn't trade it for the world.

MEMOIRS FROM PAW-PAW
by
J.E. TUMLIN "Paw-Paw"

"Upon this rock I will build my church (house)."
Matthew 16:18 (KJV)

This is an excerpt from my memoirs to my seven
grandchildren about days gone by...

I believe the Bible to be the infallible word of God. I believe that it is complete and contains no errors. I know that it has been handed down from one generation to the other. It has gone through numerous translations, yet it remains infallible. A God that can create this vast universe, (every year scientists discover that it is bigger than they thought it was the previous year) can preserve His word with His hands tied behind His back. One has serious problems when he abandons this position. Someone must decide which scriptures are correct and which are incorrect. When this happens, we are inclined to discount as incorrect those scriptures we don't like.

Paw-Paw is a "fundamentalist" or "literalist". If the scripture does not plainly indicate that it is speaking figuratively, I interpret it literally, if it makes sense. I believe we should read God's word daily and commit it to memory. Since 1978 I have read through the Bible annually. Before I retired, I would arrive at the plant 30 minutes before work time. This is when I would have my quiet time and read my Bible. I have read through many different translations. The King James Version and the New American Standard are my favorites.

Not long after I was saved, at age 28, mother presented me with Granny Brewer's Bible. (She is my grandmother on mother's side.) Her maiden name was Samantha Nichols. The only problem was that the Bible was worn completely out. Mother gave it to me in a pillow case. Granny was an illiterate mountain woman who taught herself to read the Bible after she became an adult. If she ever attended school, it was only for a week while she was visiting her cousin. According to mother, she never read anything else. The book itself was of cheap quality (not it's contents) and Granny had just worn it out.

Mother was the recipient of this treasure because she was the baby. What do you do with something like this? It has tremendous sentimental value, but no practical value. I thanked my mom and put the Bible in the closet. In 1969, we began construction of our house on Pumpkinvine Creek. Mama and I did most of the building ourselves. We used some help like brick layers, sheet rock finishers and plumbers and I had some help with the framing. We could have done the plumbing ourselves, but we were getting tired and we paid $300 to have it done.

I hired Tommy Meadows to help me lay the cement blocks for the foundation. (He really didn't help long.) Tommy and my son Rusty were present when I wrapped Granny's Bible in heavy plastic and placed it in the foundation of our house. (Upon this rock I will build my church...my house -Mt. 16:18)

I placed it on the East side of the house. We are told that our Lord will return from the East to rapture His church. I thought Granny might want to take her Bible with her to Glory. If so, she can pick it up in the sight of our Lord.

Fast forward to 1985 when we were building the new sanctuary at Tabernacle. I related what I had done with Granny's Bible to Gene Lewis (builder, good friend and member of Tabernacle) and to John Yarborough, our pastor. I suggested to them that we place a copy of God's word in the foundation of our church. They were able to get former pastor (1924) George Crowe's Bible and place it in the foundation directly under the pulpit! We're always proud to tell visiting preachers that they are standing on God's word. Come to think of it, Mama and I LIVE on God's word.

In recent years, when we have had guests for dinner or supper, I will often tell the story of Granny's Bible. I inform them that because of God and His Word, we have always considered our home to be

Holy. At the burning bush, God instructed Moses to remove his shoes from his feet because the ground on which he was standing was Holy.

I tell them this is Holy ground to me, and as High Priest of the household, in honor of God and His Word and as an act of worship, I am going to remove my shoes while I eat. I invite them to do likewise if they would like to. I tell them that if it makes them uncomfortable, don't do it. Few refuse.

Note: We were having a Sunday School Christmas party at our house and a couple arrived late. They waited almost an hour before they got up enough nerve to ask why everyone had their shoes off.

JOINING GOD IN HIS WORK
by
ANN WOOD

❦

"You intended to harm me, but God intended it for good to accomplish what is now being done, the saving of many lives."
Genesis 50:20

On August 28, 2001 my direction in life changed. In my office at work the Lord got my attention with one of those thoughts that was not my thought.

As a Wellness Director at a senior adult residential ministry, my attention had been primarily on the physical aspect of wellness-equipping and directing a wellness center, leading exercise classes, speaking on various health related topics, and supervising activities and nursing. When God spoke, He indicated I knew the spiritual/ eternal was more important than the physical. It was like being given my own personal invitation to be a part of the Great Commission right there.

The next few years would prove to be very exciting as the Lord just opened my eyes to His work. However, when asking to move to a higher plane in my walk with the Lord, I discounted the opposition as well as the sifting that this would bring.

Life remained relatively calm for the next few months. Several friends and I began a weekly prayer group. I took the *Experiencing God* study at church-then took it again-and studied it with my boss at work. I finally led the study with my prayer group. In this study Dr. Henry Blackaby teaches that God is always at work around us. We are to look and see where He is working and join Him. And this is exactly what I was invited to do.

On vacation the next summer the Lord kept leading me to read **Genesis 50:20**: *"You intended to harm me, but God intended it for good to accomplish what is now being done, the saving of many lives."* Things at work had heated up with other staff members challenging my decisions and how I chose to run my department, so I thought the first part of that verse was what applied. But the Lord kept urging me back to that verse until I realized *"the saving of many lives"* was what I needed to see.

Upon returning to work I was met with great opposition from several staff members over my desire to lead discipleship classes for our residents. And suddenly challenges were being thrown my family's way also. Within six months time my son's (age 10 at the time) life was threatened by a man who came out of the woods onto the bike path in front of our house looking for food, my daughter left home at age 17, and then our house was robbed.

In the midst of all this turmoil I did begin leading discipleship classes at work. (I had the privilege of leading 17 discipleship classes in the next three and a half years before I left that job!) I don't know that *"many lives were saved,"* but this allowed everyone who attended to hear the plan of salvation. The Wellness Center was a place of peace where residents could find a listening ear.

My boss who studied *Experiencing God* with me became one of my best friends, supporters, and prayer partners. We were both put there *"for such a time as this"* (**Esther 4:14**). We had many other stories of God at work within this broad overview of a story.

God's results: All the troublemakers at work resigned, retired, or were transferred to another facility. My son never even thought much about that crazy incident with that crazy man, once he realized we were not upset that he gave away his new book bag and some food. After some tumultuous times, my daughter and boyfriend moved to Alabama and got married. We are the proud grandparents of two- going on three-lovely grandchildren. We recovered my husband's truck that was taken in the break-in just days after it was stolen.

Just weeks after the last of the "naysayers" resigned, God released me from that job using **Joshua 22:3-4** *"...you have carried out the mission the LORD your God gave you...return to your homes..."*

God had used me to shepherd and counsel residents and to be a witness to staff and residents alike and my job was done.

I wish I could say I came through this whole ordeal trusting in the Lord and leaning not on my own understanding (see **Proverbs 3:5-6**), but there was some intense sifting that occurred along the way. The Lord dealt with me on pride and arrogance and forgiveness. I came out rather like Elijah running from Jezebel (see **I Kings 19**) trailing some anger, frustration, and bitterness. But God is faithful. He moved us to Bartow County, and I did return to my home rather than hold an outside job. And living here has provided the needed rest and recovery time.

That personal invitation to be a part of the Great Commission was not just at that job, it was for life. Just a few days ago I picked up the book, *Think Like Jesus* by George Barna. On page 26 he writes," It seems that millions of people who accept Jesus as their Savior never really accept Him as their Lord…" I have to believe this is where our challenge lies and where my challenge was in the work that I have described here. To God be the glory!

APPENDIX

HOW TO EVALUATE AND SECURE YOUR SALVATION

The following is adapted from an article written by **Billy Graham**, the most well known teacher and preacher of God's Word during our day. Please use this time to examine yourself. This could be the most important day of your life.

"The Scripture teaches that there are three kinds of people.

FIRST – There is the natural man or woman. The Bible says, "The natural man does not receive the things of the Spirit of God, for they are foolishness to him; nor can he know them, because they are spiritually discerned" (I Corinthians 2:14)

The Bible teaches us that every person born into the world is born in sin and is by nature a child of wrath. We are all separated from God and in ourselves are utterly helpless, even though this natural person often puts up a religious front and endeavors by his or her own effort to please God. Natural men and women may pray and go to church. They may be religious, but often their religion is a religion of works – of living a 'good life', of doing their best.

The Bible distinctly teaches that none of us can improve our fallen nature. We cannot, by ourselves and in ourselves and of ourselves, please God. No amount of prayer, no amount of good acts, can cause us to be acceptable in the sight of God. The natural person may be learned, able, cultured, refined and – so far as natural gifts are developed – a magnificent specimen of humanity. But the natural person, according to the Word of God, is utterly incapable of either knowing or understanding the things of God. There is only one thing natural men and women can do: repent of their sins and turn by faith to Jesus Christ.

SECOND – There is a group called carnal Christians. The apostle Paul says in I Corinthians 3:1, "I brethren, could not speak to you as to spiritual people but as to carnal, as to babes in Christ." Carnal Christians are people who (have made a decision for Christ, but) continually grieve the Holy Spirit (and those around them) by their temper, touchiness, irritability, prayerlessness, love of self, etc. These are signs of carnality, of spiritual babyhood. These people are living a worldly life void of the power of God.

THIRD – There are spiritual Christians. The person who is indwelt by the Holy Spirit, the Scripture indicates, understands spiritual truth. Spiritual men or women may not have a college education, yet they may know more about God than an unregenerate professor or an unsanctified unconsecrated theological leader. To the spiritual Christian, a whole realm of spiritual knowledge is opened up, of which the world knows nothing and the worldly Christian can only faintly imagine.

The question is this: **How can the carnal Christian become a spiritual Christian?**

There was a time, perhaps, when you were a spiritual Christian. You still had your first love; a fire burned in your heart for God. But something has happened along the way, something has disturbed your relationship with God, and you no longer know the joy, the peace and the thrill that you once knew. You do not take time to read your Bible. Your prayer times are few. Your interest in spiritual things has waned, and yet there is a great hungering after God, an aching in your soul for the joy and victory that you have seen in the lives of others. You want that joy in *your* soul, that thrill in *your* heart. You want to know the power of prayer again.

The Bible teaches that you can have glorious, daily victory. Scripture says, *"For sin shall not have dominion over you, for you are not under law but under grace"* **(Romans 6:14)....**In **Romans 8:2** we read, *"For the law of the Spirit of life in Christ Jesus has made me free from the law of sin and death."* And in **I Corinthians 15:57**, *"But thanks be to God, who gives us victory through our Lord Jesus Christ."*...

Backsliding and carnality are inexcusable (and do not have to be) part of the normal Christian experience...Since the living Christ dwells within every one of us who has accepted Him as Savior, there is never any reason for defeat. No enemy is too powerful for Christ! Every temptation may be resisted!

If you as a Christian are overcome by the enemy, the simple explanation is that Christ has been denied His rightful position of supremacy in your heart. **The dethronement of Christ will always lead to failure** in spiritual warfare. It is Christ, and Christ alone, who can give you constant, daily, victorious life."

Billy Graham continues...

"The Bible teaches that every Christian has 3 enemies:

First – The world. This means the present evil world and the great system of evil around us. (This includes) everything around us that has a tendency to lead us into sin.

It can mean the evil people of the world or the things of the world.

Certain elements of daily life are not sinful in themselves, but they can lead to sin if they are abused. Abuse means 'extreme use" or overuse... (For example) making money is necessary for daily living. But money-making is apt to degenerate into money-loving...which will spoil our spiritual life. The Bible admonishes, *"Do not love the world or the things in the world."* **(I John 2:15)**

Second – The flesh. Paul said, *"I know that in me (that is, in my flesh) nothing good dwells"* **(Romans 7:18)** The Bible teaches that the flesh is fallen human nature. It is…sin, the carnal nature that (we all) have inherited from our parents. The flesh is the birthplace of all those ugly sins that mar our Christian joy and hinder our testimony. The sins of temper, irritability, moodiness, jealousy, pride, selfishness, an unforgiving spirit, anxiety and fretfulness, harshness, complaining, criticism, lust – all of these things characterize the flesh.

Third – The devil. Referred to by Paul as *'the prince of the air'* **(Ephesians 2:2)**

The Bible teaches that the devil is a real person. His objective is to defeat the will of God in the world, the church and the Christian. He is the unceasing enemy of the soul. He must be met and overcome. Thank God, through the victory of Jesus Christ on the cross, this mighty enemy has been fully and finally vanquished! One day…the whole world will see Christ's triumph. Meanwhile, Satan is busy in the world, sometimes appearing as an angel of light **(II Corinthians 11:14),** and other times as a roaring lion, "seeking whom he may devour" **(I Peter 5:8).**

These, then, are our three foes: the world, the flesh and the devil. The attitude of every Christian to all three of them is summed up in one word: *renounce.* There must be no bargaining, no compromise, no hesitation. Absolute renunciation is the only possible way for the Christian to have victory in your life…

If you are still a 'natural man or woman' – if you have never known the joy and peace that Jesus gives – you can be forgiven if you will turn from your sin and by faith accept Christ as Lord and Savior. Why not turn to Him right now? You can pray something like this: [1]

> **God, I am a sinner. I'm sorry for my sin. I realize I can have no forgiveness and no victory apart from You. Forgive me. I want to turn from my sin. I receive Jesus Christ as my Savior; I confess Him as my Lord. From now on, I want to follow Him. Help me to listen to You, yield my way to You, and obey You from this day forward. In Jesus' name,**
>
> **Amen.**

If you prayed that prayer, welcome into the family of God! You are a new person. A new creation according to **II Corinthians 5:17** *"Therefore, if anyone is in Christ, he is a new creation; the old has gone, the new has come!"*

We encourage you to write this day down and to tell someone about your decision, maybe the person who gave you this book.

If you do not have a church home, we want to invite you to join us here at Tabernacle Baptist Church in Cartersville, Georgia. If you live outside of Cartersville, we encourage you to find a Bible believing church in your area.

The Bible teaches that baptism is the next step after salvation. This is very important. It is an outward sign of an inward decision. Don't delay! Call your pastor today or call us here at Tabernacle and we will be happy to set that up for you. We also want to encourage you to get plugged-in to Sunday School at your church or to one of the many classes we have here at Tabernacle. We would love to have you! **(770-382-1977)**

Today, this _____ day of _____, 20_____, I made the decision to turn from my sin and follow Christ. I am, by faith, a new creation with a new life!

Printed in the United States
96195LV00002B/217-399/A